BUSINESS PROCESS RE-ENGINEERING IN COMMERCIAL BANKS :

A CASE STUDY OF STATE BANK OF HYDERABAD

Prof. S.V. SATYANARAYANA
M.Com, M.Phil, Ph.D
Professor of Commerce,
Officer on Special Duty to the Vice-Chancellor,
Osmania University, Hyderabad.

And

Dr. (Mrs.) N.V. KAVITHA
M.Com, M.Phil, Ph.D
Dean, Administration,
Head, Department of Commerce,
St.Ann's College for Women, Mehdipatnam, Hyderabad.

Himalaya Publishing House

MUMBAI • NEW DELHI • NAGPUR • BANGALORE • HYDERABAD • CHENNAI • PUNE • LUCKNOW • AHMEDABAD • ERNAKULAM • BHUBANESWAR • INDORE

FIRST EDITION : 2011

Published by : Mrs. Meena Pandey
for **HIMALAYA PUBLISHING HOUSE PVT. LTD.,**
"Ramdoot", Dr. Bhalerao Marg, Girgaon, **Mumbai - 400 004.**
Phones: 2386 01 70/2386 38 63, Fax: 022-2387 71 78
Email: himpub@vsnl.com
Website: www.himpub.com

Branch Offices:

New Delhi :
New Delhi - 110 002. Phone: 23270392, 23278631, Fax: 011-23256286

Nagpur : Kundanlal Chandak Industrial Estate, Ghat Road, **Nagpur - 440 018.**
Phone: 2738731, 3296733 Telefax : 0712-2721215

Bangalore : No. 16/1 (Old 12/1), 1st Floor, Next to Hotel Highlands,
Madhava Nagar, Race Course Road, **Bangalore - 560 001.**
Phone : 22281541, 22385461, Telefax: 080-22286611

Hyderabad : No. 3-4-184, Lingampally, Besides Raghavendra Swamy Matham,
Kachiguda, **Hyderabad - 500 027.** Phone: 040-27550139
Mobile : 09848130433

Chennai : No. 85/50, Bazullah Road, T. Nagar, **Chennai - 600 017.**
Phone: 044-28144004/28144005

Pune :
(Near Prabhat Theatre), **Pune - 411 030.**
Phone: 020-24496323/24496333

Lucknow : C-43, Sector - C, Ali Gunj, **Lucknow - 226 024.** Phone: 0522-2339329

Ahmedabad : 114, "SHAIL", 1st Floor, Opp. Madhu Sudan House, C.G.Road,
Navrang Pura, **Ahmedabad – 380 009.**
Phone: 079-26560126, Mobiles: 09327324149,09314679413

Ernakulam : 39/104 A, Lakshmi Apartment, Karikkamuri Cross Rd.,
Ernakulam, **Cochin – 622011**, Kerala.
Phone: 0484-2378012, 2378016, Mob.: 09344199799

Bhubaneswar : 5 Station Square, **Bhubaneswar (Orissa) - 751 001.**
Mobile: 9861046007, E-mail:- orissa@himpub.com

Indore : Kesardeep Avenue Extension, 73, Narayan Bagh.Flat No. 302, IIIrd
Floor, Near Humpty Dumpty School, Narayan Bagh, **Indore (M.P.)**
Mobile: 09301386468

DTP by : **Vani Graphics, Hyderabad.**

Printed by : **Sri Bala Offset Printers,** Hyderabad

ACKNOWLEDGEMENT

We gratefully acknowledge the support, guidance and contributions of all our friends and well-wishers, who have made this book possible.

UNIT - III

LIST OF TABLES

UNIT - IV

UNIT - V

LIST OF CHARTS

UNIT – II

LIST OF ABBREVATIONS

SCB's	Scheduled Commercial Banks
PSB'S	Public Sector Banks
NPLs	Non -Performing loans
IT	Information Technology
BPR	Business Process Re-engineering
SBH	State Bank of Hyderabad
ALM	Asset-liability management
CBS	Core Banking Solution
OLAP	On-line analytic processing
EDI	Electronic Data Interchange
RM	Relationship Manager
HLST	Home loan sales team
MPST	Multi-product sales team
CST	combined sales team
CPC	Central Processing Centres
RACPC	Retail Assets Central Processing Centres
SMECC	Small and Medium Enterprise credit centre
CAC	Currency Administration Cell
CPPC	Centralized Pension Processing Centre
TFCPC	Trade finance CPC
SARC	Stressed Assets Resolution Centre
GNPA'	Gross Non Performing assets
NNPA	Net Non Performing assets
BPE	Business per employee
PPE	Profit per employee
APE	Advances per employee
DPE	Deposits per employee
(CAR)	Capital Adequacy Ratio
VRS	Voluntary Retirement service

CONTENTS

CHAPTER – I

INTRODUCTION

"It is not the strongest of the species that survives, or the most intelligent; it is the one that is most adaptable to change" **– *Charles Darwin***

Banking sector has remained the backbone of Indian economy since independence. Since the early 1960's major changes have taken place in the environment in which banks conduct their business. Some of these changes in the banking environment are due to macroeconomic trends, globalization, deregulation, advancement in technology, increasing competition, and disintermediation.

The intensified challenges and increased complexities of contemporary Indian banking make it necessary to put in place measures, such as, spread management, rapid technological up gradation, product innovation, business process reengineering (BPR), check on transaction cost and reduction of impaired assets to make the growth in profits sustainable over the long haul. Banks need to put in place a comprehensive business model to promote real time simulation for a healthy, efficient, sound and internationally competitive banking system.

Currently, India has 88 scheduled commercial banks (SCBs) - 28 public sector banks (that is with the Government of India holding a stake), 29 private banks (these do not have government stake; they may be publicly listed and traded on stock exchanges) and 31 foreign banks. They have a combined network of over 67,000 branches and 17,000 ATMs. According to a report by ICRA Limited, a rating agency, the public sector banks hold over 75 % of total assets of the banking industry, with the private and foreign banks holding 18.2% and 6.5% respectively.

Banking in India is considered as fairly mature in terms of supply, product range and reach-even though reach in rural India still remains a challenge for the private sector and foreign banks. Even in terms of quality of assets and capital adequacy, Indian banks are considered to have clean, strong and transparent balance sheets-as compared to other banks in developed economies.

In a way Business Process Re-Engineering is a' transformation' as opposed to 'change', that alters the basic rhythm and character of the organization. In the present economic scenario it is inevitable for any bank to perform without reengineering their processes, irrespective of the nature of the bank (public sector bank, private or foreign banks). Thereby a study has been undertaken to study the impact of BPR on commercial banks.

Business Process Reengineering (BPR) entails modification in the existing rules and procedures to attain a higher level of operational efficiency and better internal controls. Diversification and the rapid change have become the distinguishing features of the banking industry. The prime objective of BPR is to align business processes with automation and the 'best practices' available in the field / market. The BPR is not a one time solution rather it is a continuous process of screening and re-engineering / modification to bring about excellence in the service delivery to stakeholders.

The chapter is divided into two parts, Part 'A' consists of a brief discussion about progress and trends of Indian banking sector. In Part 'B' explains the need and importance of the study, its objectives and scope. Period of the study, sources of data, research methodology adopted, and organization of study, limitations, and review of literature are also presented.

PART – A

1.1 Banking System in India

The banking system in India is significantly different from that of other Asian nations because of the country's unique geographic, social, and economic characteristics. India has a large population and land size, a diverse culture, and extreme disparities in income, which are marked among its regions. There are high levels of illiteracy among a large percentage of its population but, at the same time, the country has a large reservoir of managerial and technologically advanced talents. Between about 30 and 35 percent of the population resides in metro and urban cities and the rest is spread in several semi-urban and rural centers. The country's economic policy framework combines socialistic and capitalistic features with a heavy bias towards public sector investment. India has followed the path of growth-led exports rather than the "export-led growth" of other Asian economies, with emphasis on self-reliance through import substitution.

These features are reflected in the structure, size, and diversity of the country's banking and financial sector. The banking system has had to serve the goals of economic policies enunciated in successive five- year development plans, particularly concerning equitable income distribution, balanced regional economic growth, and the reduction and elimination of private sector monopolies in trade and industry. In order for the banking industry to serve as an instrument of state policy, it was subjected to various nationalization schemes in different phases (1955, 1969, and 1980). As a result, banking remained internationally isolated (few Indian banks had presence abroad in international financial centers) because of preoccupations with domestic priorities, especially massive branch expansion and attracting more people to the system. Moreover, the sector has been as signed the role of providing support to other economic sectors such as agriculture, small-scale industries, exports, and banking activities in the developed commercial centers (i.e., metro, urban, and a limited number of semi-urban centers).

The banking system's international isolation was also due to strict branch licensing controls on foreign banks already operating in the country as well as entry restrictions facing new foreign banks. A criterion of reciprocity is required for any Indian bank to open an office abroad.

1.2 Progress and trends in Indian Banking Sector

The Indian Banking industry, which is governed by the Banking Regulation Act of India, 1949 can be broadly classified into two major categories, non-scheduled banks and scheduled banks. Scheduled banks comprise commercial banks and the co-operative banks. In terms of ownership, commercial banks can be further grouped into nationalized banks, the State Bank of India and its group banks, regional rural banks and private sector banks (the old/new domestic and foreign).

During the six decades since independence, banking in India has evolved through four distinct phases. The first phase of financial reforms resulted in the nationalization of 14 major banks in 1969 and resulted in a shift from Class banking to Mass banking. This in turn resulted in a significant growth in the geographical coverage of banks. Every bank had to earmark a minimum percentage of their loan portfolio to sectors identified as "priority sectors". The manufacturing sector also grew during the 1970s in protected environs and the banking sector was a critical source. The next wave of reforms saw the nationalization of 6 more commercial banks in 1980. Since then the number of scheduled commercial banks increased four-fold and the number of bank branches increased eight-fold.

After the second phase of financial sector reforms and liberalization of the sector in the early nineties, the Public Sector Banks (PSB) found it extremely difficult to compete with the new private sector banks and the foreign banks. The new private sector banks first made their appearance after the guidelines permitting them were issued in January 1993. Eight new private sector banks are presently in operation. These banks due to their late start have access to state-of-the-art technology, which in turn helps them to save on manpower costs and provide better services.

The industry is currently in a transition phase. On the one hand, the PSBs, which are the mainstay of the Indian Banking system, are in the process of reducing the costs in terms of excessive manpower, excessive Non Performing Assets (NPAs) and excessive governmental equity, while on the other hand the private sector banks are consolidating themselves through mergers and acquisitions.

Public Sector banks are forced to adopt new concepts in banking, turn tech savvy, and obtain more autonomy by keeping governmental stake to the minimum. They can succeed in effectively taking on the private sector banks by virtue of their sheer size. Weaker PSU banks are unlikely to survive in the long run. Consequently, they are likely to be either acquired by stronger players or will be forced to look out for other strategies to infuse greater capital and optimize their operations.

During Fourth phase, also called as Reform Phase, Recommendations of the Narasimham Committee (1991) paved the way for the reform phase in the banking sector. Entry of new banks resulted in a paradigm shift in the ways of banking in India. The increasing and growing expectations led to increased awareness amongst banks on the role and importance of technology in banking. The arrival of foreign and private banks with their superior state-of-the-art technology-based services pushed Indian banks also to follow suit by going in for the latest technologies so as to deal with the threat of competition and retain their customer base.

For the service sector, sustaining long-term customer relationship management (CRM) has become a challenge with almost every player in the market offering similar products. With productivity, efficiency and profitability gaining currency as a 'mantra' for banks in the present day context, the pricing of products, be it deposit or advance has become more complex. Here IT comes to the rescue of banking sector.

As the Basel II Capital Accord continues to evolve it requires banks to implement a comprehensive risk framework across the institution. One of the key challenges which the banks are facing in the implementation of the Basel II is the assimilation of new processes and reengineering of existing processes.

Information Technology has basically been used in two different avenues in Banking. One is Communication and Connectivity and other is Business Process Reengineering. Information technology enables sophisticated product development, better market infrastructure, implementation of reliable techniques for control of risks and helps the financial intermediaries to reach geographically distant and diversified markets.

1.3 *Issues Facing the Indian Banking Sector

The Indian Banking sector is facing five major issues namely :

1. **Competition** : The Indian banking sector is highly competitive, with both private and public institutions competing across a range of financial products. Much of this competition stems from the growth of the individual consumer as a force in the marketplace. Private Banks were the most aggressive at servicing this segment and forced the concept of customer

service into the fore. And thus public sector banks begin to make the investments necessary to compete on a more equal footing

2. **Youth population :** India enjoys a favorable demographic position with a large young, employed population. These young people are not averse to taking loans, and their rising income levels make them more attractive targets for banks. The private banks excelled in penetrating and marketing to this target group, and this has helped drive retail lending.

3. **Margin pressures :** Banks are trying to diversify through other products such as credit cards and personal loans, but competition is fierce. The cost of deposits has also been going up in the face of competition from the mutual fund and insurance industries. On the corporate side, things look a little better, with higher margins and low nonperforming loans (NPLs).

4. **Government securities :** Beyond the more traditional banking services, all Indian banks are required to keep a minimum of 25% of their net deposits in government securities. Many banks operate significantly above these levels, and are keen to reduce these positions; others are reluctant to do so. The profitability of these treasury operations has been relatively predictable, but the low margins and risk of rate rises are of concern.

5. **Foreign Institutions :** Foreign players are getting more aggressive in India and have expanded both organically and through acquisition. HSBC and ING have made investments in domestic firms, and many others are waiting for opportunities to do so. Foreign investment limits have been raised, but there are still restrictions on market entry. If the government ever elects to privatize the public banks, foreign players would likely be keen to pick up stakes.

*** Source : Financial Insights, 2005**

1.4 Review of literature

The studies conducted on Business process reengineering in commercial banks are few in number, since it is relatively new phenomenon started after 2000. Hence an attempt is made to review the research work done in commercial banking in general and BPR in commercial banking in particular.

Aggarwal, (1979), [1] conducted a study on nationalized banks with special reference to their social obligations. The main recommendations of the study were : (i) providing more branch office to the public particularly in the semi-urban and rural areas and in the lead districts, (ii) providing greater credit facilities to the public as well as to the priority and neglected sectors, (iii) facilitating and maintenance of employment opportunities in the country, (iv) financing the government securities and (v) popularizing the bill form of credit.

Adhivarahan, (2001), [2] his article is a humble attempt to have a bird's eye view of the provisions of the Act and the pros and cons of the provisions of the Act with particular reference to the activities of banks. The study concludes that the number of incidents of e-fraud and on-line breaches is the highest in India. Therefore Cyber crimes in banking sector have to be treated with more care. For this purpose, Statutory Body similar to "Internet Fraud Center" should be formed in India.

Amandeep, (1983), [3] studies various factors which affect the profitability of commercial banks with the help of multiple regression analysis. She has tried to determine the share of each factor which determines the profitability of commercial banks. The trend analysis, ratio analysis, multiple regression analysis was effectively used to study the profitability of commercial banks.

Angadi & Devraj, (1983) [4] the studies were mainly based on published financial statements instead of their break-up. These authors observed that besides the social responsibilities discharged by the public sector bank, deficiencies, ineffective mobilization of funds at lower costs, attractive retail banking augmenting earnings from other sources, effective cash and portfolio management has contributed to declaration in productivity and profitability of banks.

Avasthi, and Sharma, (2000-2001), [5] advances in technology are set to change the face of the banking business. Technology is set to change the face of the banking business. Technology has transformed both the delivery channels used by banks in retail banking. It has also greatly impacted the entire banking sector. Both the authors explored the challenges that the banking industry and its regulators face.

B. Janki, (2002), [6] analyzed in her article that how technology is effecting employee's productivity. There is no doubt, in India particularly; PSBs need to use technology to improve operating efficiency and customer services. Harnessing employee technology synergy is crucial for unleashing productivity and reaching out to the huge base of retail customers, who are also dispersed in rural and semi-urban areas. Banks can use technology to address customer needs and improve their interaction with customers keeping in touch through telephone and Internet. The focus on technology will increase like never before to add value to customer service, develop new products, strengthen risk management, and asset liability management and improve profitability. However technology is only an enabling tool and whether banks actually achieve what they want to achieve will be determined by the drive and motivation of their work force and response of the staff.

Bajaj, (2000), [7] highlighted e-commerce related issues due to the adoption of recent trends in IT. All over the world, bank's traditional business of taking advances and lending out the proceeds is in terminal decline. The spread of IT and the dramatic advances in financial theory have made it cheaper for big companies to raise money in the capital markets than from banks. IT is also helping in cutting costs by providing cheaper ways of delivering products to customers. ATMs, telephone banking and now the Internet banking. He also explained e-commerce, payment systems, smart card, and electronic cheque etc. He concluded that electronic payment systems are emerging and getting accepted in the market place. They need to gain both consumer and business acceptance. But the major point that emerges from the above discussion is that banking stands to radically change. It remains to be seen whether banks use e-commerce and other IT systems to reinvent themselves, gain access to new markets or they become extinct.

Bajaj, (1999), [8] Information and IT are the key drivers of the Information Age, also referred to as the post industrial society. The Information Age has ushered in a knowledge-based industrial revolution. The business in this era is networked and uses IT to survive in a highly competitive environment. The relationship between IT and business is discussed in this article and it is explained how IT affects business.

Banton, (1990), [9] explains that the introduction of IT, has positively affected the productivity, profitability and efficiency of banks. But many bank frauds are also taking place. They are the hidden threat to financial institutions. He analyzed the mechanism as to how bank frauds are taking place and how to tackle them.

Bhasin, (2001), [10] has analyzed the impact of IT on banking sector. The IT has revolutionised various aspects of our life. It has transformed the repetitive and overlapping systems and procedures, into simple single key pressing technology resulting in speed, accuracy and efficiency in conducting the business. The computerization of banks has provided a major push for enabling them to enter into the newer activities. The banking industry has prepared itself and is strongly emerging to play a major supplementary role in nurturing e-commerce applications which is still in the infancy stage in India. While few of the new generation private banks have taken an early initiative in these innovative areas, other banks are gradually catching up. The author feels that it is of utmost importance that proper security infrastructure should be in place for routing transactions through the public network.

Bhattacharya (1977), [11] studies the impact of the limited liberalization initiated before the deregulation of the nineties on the performance of the different categories of banks, using Data Envelopment analysis. His study covered 70 banks in the period 1986-91. He constructed one grant frontier for the entire period and measured technical efficiency of banks under study. They found PSBs had the highest efficiency among the three categories with foreign and private banks having much lower efficiencies. However PSBs started showing a decline in efficiency after 1987, private banks showed no change and foreign banks showed sharp rise in efficiency. The main results were in accord with the general perception that in the nationalized era, public sector banks were successful in achieving their principal objective of deposit and loan expansion.

Bhuia, (2000), [12] explained the future of Internet. According to him, a few people are predicting the death of the Internet due to burgeoning traffic. However no signs of this are in evidence even as the number of Internet users has grown exponentially. In fact, the myriad services have improved with enhanced technologies and superior interfaces.

Bilgrarni, (1982), [13] conducted a study on the banking growth imbalances over a decade since nationalization in branch expansion, deposit mobilization, credit disbursement and priority sector lending. The study concludes that although regional and state-wise disparities in terms of banking services still exist, some healthy trends were developed significantly and if continued in future, would further help in minimizing the widening gaps.

Birla Institute of Scientific Research, [14] conducted a study to evaluate the performance of nationalized banks in comparison with that of banks in private sector. The emphasis of the study was on the objectives of nationalization and their achievements, relative performance of private sector banks and nationalized banks since 1969 and the effect of nationalization on rest of the banking sector. The study reveals that the growth and development in banking after nationalization was not just because of transfer of ownership. It was rather because various incentives and punitive measures were implemented with more vigilance and care after 1969 by the government and the Reserve Bank of India to makes bank fulfill their social responsibilities. Similarly in same spheres even better results were achieved by non-nationalized banks. The performance of private sector banks in the post-nationalization period was noteworthy, especially because of the odds they faced in securing the growth of the business. The achievement of significantly high growth in deposits, advances, and branches etc. clearly showed the high quality of entrepreneurship and management of these banks.

Brett, (1977), [15] studied the changing old money structure into E-Money. Now the banks are providing different cards to their customers. The E-Money can be used at any time to pay for goods and services. The coins and bank notes are replaced by digitally signed files. The advantage of this system is that the cost of passing on the money is nearly zero. He emphasized that it is necessary to study the financial management in the electronic age.

Chakrabarthy, (1986), [16] made a modest attempt to access empirically the relative performance of each bank in the context of three variable viz. profit earnings and expenses. In his study, Herfindha's index has been computed to measure the inequality in the sharing of profits, net profits, earnings and expenses by each group of banker. The author has suggested that each scheduled commercial bank should take up some exercise to evaluate the relative performance of each office of the particular bank for profit planning.

Chopra, (1987), [17] in her study devoted a chapter to productivity in which she analyzed productivity of five selected national banks. However the results were highly unreliable as the same were based on figures at current prices.

Clifford, (1996), [18] studies the impact of IT on the financial services. Due to the introduction of IT, the role of banks, mutual funds, & insurance companies are changing. The banks will never be the same again. The dimensions of banking business are changing the new economy.

Das, (1999), [19] compares performance among public sector banks for three years in the post-reform period, 1992, 1995 and 1998. He finds a certain convergence in performance. He also notes that while there is a welcome increase in emphasis on non-interest income, banks have tended to show risk-averse behavior by opting for risk-free investments over risky loans.

David O'Sullivan, (1996), [20] examines Business process re-engineering tools which offer, techniques to model the enterprise and identify opportunities to make change. He explains the approaches, tools and techniques which support redesign the enterprise in achieving world-class performance.

Federick & Phil, (2000), [21] analyzed the aspect of E-Loyalty. With the introduction of IT, it has created many doubts and questions. In the rush to build Internet business, many executives concentrate all their attention on attracting customers rather than retaining them. According to them, the unique economics of e-business make customer loyalty more important than ever.

Godse, (1983), [22] he suggested certain indicators of productivity which may be used at various levels of management in a bank. He further made suggestions towards improvement of productivity.

Gupta and Goswami, (1986), [23] in their study introduced some radical change in measuring profitability of commercial banks. They indicated that the major cause for declining profitability is the enormous increase in establishment costs. The author pointed out that the conventional indications are based on published profits, which do not reflect the true position. The author therefore suggested an alternative measure, based on the cost of mobilizing business, other things being equal elasticity of establishment costs (per unit of business) with respect to staff strength.These may be used to compare the operational efficiency (and thereby profitability) of different banks.

Guy Doumeingts, (1985), [24] in his book deals with the striving of present enterprises to improve their competitiveness in a changing environment. The author is of the opinion that the companies have to evaluate their performances by combining modelling, business process re-engineering and benchmarking techniques to reach the objectives. This book demonstrates the successful combination and implementation of these various techniques.

Heggade, (2000), [25] his work analyzed the banker-customer relationship in the Indian PSBs. It is a unique work since it analysis the wide range of customer services provided by banks and the role of bank staff in its delivering. Further it analyzes the bank customer needs and the extent of the use of the customer services and brings out the fact that the enormous increase in the work load in banks on account of social banking has lead to their poor quality of services. This study makes out a case for pricing appropriately all types of bank services and enhances their quality. It also critically analyzes the recommendations of Saraiya Committee, Talwar Committee and Goiporia Committee on improving the range and quality of customer services in banks. He has distributed bank customers in eleven parts (Business, Salaries Class, Advocates, and Peasants. Doctors, Nurses, Small Scale Industrialists, Transport Operators, Self Employed, Engineers, Others) and all the banks in four parts (PSBs, Private Sector Banks, Co-operative banks and Rural banks).

Hussain, (1988), [26] also highlighted the importance of IT in various sectors. In the introduction of any new technology or system various organizational, financial & functional problems are faced in the initial stages, People are generally reluctant to accept new system, howsoever beneficial it may be. Such various issues which are involved in computerization have been critically & vividly discussed.

Hui-Liang Tsai,(1987),[27] The author takes an integrated approach to the discussion of organizational learning, new value propositions, supply-chain optimization, e-commerce, new perspectives on business process reengineering, collaborative business models, globalization of business, and the continuing trend toward virtual integration. He feels that utilizing technology alone to its full potential is not sufficient but it should be supported by overhauling the rigid, hierarchical business model that was designed for the command-and-control corporate environment of the industrial era.. A more synchronized supply chain yields better customer service, higher quality, faster delivery, and lower inventory.

Johri & Jauhari, (1994), [28] also analyzed the importance of computers in banking industry. They also analyzed various issues related to computerization in banks in India. They emphasized on the need for banks to use e-commerce and other IT systems to reinvest themselves, gain access to new markets or they become extinct.

Joshi (1986), [29] the contribution of the author indicated various reasons for declining trends in profitability. His study is based on published data. He has suggested profits planning both at micro & macro levels for the banking industry to overcome the declining trends in profitability.

Karkal, (1982), [30] he examines the concept of profit & profitability, and the factors that determines the volume or magnitude of profits and the techniques used in profit planning. He has suggested certain measures to improve the profitability in banks through increasing the margin between lending (advances) and borrowing (deposits) rates, improving the profitability of staff, and implementation of a uniform service charge. The study did not touch up the area of cost of banking services, the costing exercises in the banking industry.

Kaveri, (2001), [31] this study attempts to extend the study conducted by the Verma Committee more specifically to ascertain whether enough signals of weakness were indicated much before the event. This study considers 1998-99 as the year of event when the Verma Committee identified weak banks, strong banks and potential weak banks. This study considers seven efficiency parameters which are computed, based on the data collected from the Reserve Bank of India publications. The parameters include:

- Net Non Performance Assets/Net Adequacy.
- Net Profit/Total Assets.
- Gross Profit/Working Funds.
- Net Interest Income/Total Assets.
- Interest Expended/Total Assets.
- Intermediation Cost/Total Assets.
- Provisions and Contingencies/Total Assets.

The above parameters focus on two major concerns of banks i.e. loan default and profitability whereas the Verma Committee covered all aspects of financial health. This study has given some evidence to indicate that no bank can be weak or potential weak all of a sudden. There is a gradual deterioration in the position of loan default &

profitability. Hence it is suggested to develop a ratio model to arrive at a single score to classify banks into three categories i.e. weak, strong and potential weak.

Kohli, (2001), [32], emphasized on the importance of technology & issues emerging from technology. According to him technology is emerging as a key-driver of business in the financial services industry. The advancement in computing and telecommunications has revolutionized the financial industry and banking on the net is fast catching on. As e-commerce gets transformed into m-commerce with the increasing use of technologies like WAP, banking business is in for a major overhaul.

Kulkarni, (2000), [33] in his article attempts to review the various seminal changes which have taken place at an astonishing pace today which are likely to completely change the pace of banking like never before. The traditional brick and mortar bank is giving way to the virtual bank with e-banking leading the way. He also discussed the future scenario of banking. As the brick-and-mortar edifice of banks starts crumbling and banks enter an era of virtual banking, the barriers of geography and time would crumble and communication would just be a click away. In the above scenario the role of the traditional bank branch of the 20th century would be almost non-existence. The above scenario seems improbable at the first reading but it is very likely if one studies the fast pace of changes taking place in the advanced countries especially with the emergence of the Internet, e-commerce and revolutionary changes in telecommunications.

Mumupilly, (1980), [34] the work of these authors is a modest attempt on the cost and profitability of commercial banks in India. These studies provide an analytical view of the trends in the components of cost of earnings of different groups of Indian commercial banks since nationalization. These studies mainly focus on the cost and profitability of banking industry as a whole rather than individual bank.

Murty, (2001), [35] the author analyzed the significance of banking sector in the insurance sector. On the eve of banks entry in insurance, the study made an attempt to trace the historical background of India to private investment, banks eagerness to enter insurance market, basic mechanics of insurance, functions of a typical insurer, different kinds of insurance coverages critical component of insurance business and how prepared banks are for exploiting these new business opportunities. According to the author there are many issues to be sorted out before banks take-up insurance business. The new entrants are likely to give a stiff competition through their customized activities and usage of technology to reach the customer with minimal resistance from any quarter.

Nair, (2000), [36] the technological advancements achieved very recently in the field of computerization have unfolded many areas of innovations in our living styles. The world of banking is fast shedding its ancient image and entering from 'brick-and-mortar' model to 'click' model. The virtual banking is rising as a total revolution in the banking transactions.

The author realized that those banking and financial service providers who switch over to the electronic environment in the quickest possible time frame alone will be able to survive. The introduction of Cyber Law is also expected to boost the E-Commerce and E-Banking further in the days to come. And the writing on the wall rather on the net is clear for the Indian Banking Industry: E-Banking has come to stay.

Narayan, K. (1982), [37] conducted study on the performance evaluation of commercial banks and presented a performance evaluation model on the basis of important quantifiable parameters of performance. The main conclusions were: (I) the present system of ranking the banks on the basis of aggregate deposits failed to reflect their overall achievements: (II) the existing system of performance budgeting is not suitable at branch level; (III) on the basis of all the important and quantifiable parameters of performance, an integrated performance index needs to be developed for evaluating the performance of commercial banks.

Niranjan, (2000), [38] studied the changing business dimensions of banks due to the introduction of IT. The Internet is taking banks in directions other than loans & deposits. Banking in India will never be the same again. E-Banks have started E-Commerce and many banks are entering the insurance sector.

Ojha, (1987), [39] in his paper made an international comparison of productivity and profitability of public sector banks of India making comparisons on the basis of per-employee indicators and taking the example of State bank group and PNB noted that Indian banks are the largest in all accounts. Analysis indicated unsatisfactory position in the case of Regional Rural Banks and relatively lowers productivity in the private sector banks.

Pathrose, (2001), [40] opined that banking around the world over is undergoing a rapid and radical transformation due to the all pervasive influence of IT and breath taking developments in the technology of telecommunications and electronic data processing. The winds of change are blowing in India too. The IT which implies the integration of information system with communication technology has radically altered the traditional ways of doing banking business and allowed banks to wipe out the difference in time as well as distance. It is in this context his article attempts to trace the present status of hi-tech banking in India, visualize its prospects and look at the challenges and problems in the tracks to be traversed. He concludes that in the scenario of severe competition and escalating expectation of customers for newer products and alternative delivery channels, the contours of banking are being redefined. The key to survival of banks therefore is retention of customers loyalty by providing them with value added services tailored to their needs, using state-of-the-art IT. There is no way a bank can remain lukewarm to hi-tech and yet hope to grow. It is a choice between survival and extinction.

Prabharkar, (1986), [41] has analyzed the nature and range of customer services provide by Indian banks. He has brought out the fact that in case of Indian banks, a major portion of complaints is from depositors with the masse banking practice, a different treatment is neither possible nor permitted. The possibilities of dividing customers may be of some better service to important customers. The teller system partially serves this purpose. He has clearly brought out that in India there is a growing size of current and saving account holders who do not maintain the statutorily required minimum balances. Thus, the size of defaulters is high and growing, which would cause additional work to bankers.

R. Radhakrishnan, (2008),[42] the book offers a step-by-step presentation of the practical framework and management techniques needed to achieve engineering solutions for implementation of BPR in an organization. The initial chapters explain the need for BPR and its utility in relation to IT and manufacturing. The middle chapters cover the methodology, success factors, barriers, and the technologies that are relevant for BPR implementation. The latter chapters present solutions like lean and virtual manufacturing, enterprise resource planning, and functional information systems. An exclusive chapter is devoted to concepts and tasks of software reengineering.

Ranagarajan, (2000), [43] in his inaugural address at the 4th Bank Educationists' Conference on 6th March6, 2000 at Hyderabad, explained the importance of IT in the financial sector. At a time when banking the world over is undergoing a radical transformation due to the all pervasive influence of IT. Banking education and training must not only respond to the fast changing needs of the financial system but also become proactive and play the role of a 'Change Agent' and bring about a 'skills revolution' in the banking industry. Banks will begin to function increasingly under competitive pressures. In meeting the new challenges, the use of computer, Internet and communication technology will assume a critical role. Bank customers are becoming very demanding and it is the extensive use of technology that will enable banks to satisfy adequately the requirements of customers. The use of technology would also improve availability of information for management decisions and for monitoring operations.

Rao, (2002), [44] he analyzed the impact of new technology on banking sector. The advent of technology both in terms of computers and communications has been changing totally the ways and doing banking business. Technology has opened new vistas and in turn brought new possibilities every day for doing the same work differently and in most cost-effective manner. Tele banking and Internet banking are making forays such that branch banking may give to home banking. In order to protect their profitability, the banks need to address urgently the following emerging areas :

- Product development and marketing skills
- Modern credit management skills.
- New risk management practices.
- Skills for operating in electronic environment.
- New Internal audit skills in a changing business environment.
- New focus on customer and his needs.

Rao, (1999), [45] explained the role of IT in the financial services industry. Technology is bringing about important evolutionary changes in the investment industry, giving portfolio managers greater control of their activities and even more time to spend on developing insights into the stock they own.

Roger Maull, Stephen Childe, (1994), [46] examines the current literature surrounding business process re-engineering (BPR) in the article Business Process Re-engineering: An Example from the Banking Sector defines BPR and distinguishes between re-engineering and other change programmes. He sets out a general approach to BPR and outlines the results from the application of this approach to the bank. The analysis of results includes an assessment of the applicability of the ICAM definition method, IDEF0, in helping companies implement BPR programme.

Roger, (2000), [47] feels that a set of principles can actually prevent most fires in business. Pretty much everyone acknowledges that business is being completely reinvented because transaction costs are much lower on the Internet than in traditional channels. The banks are rapidly shifting their business functions and customers relationships on to the Web.

Sabnani, (2000), [48] he analyzed the importance of "Universal Banking" in India. Globalization, Liberalization and Deregulation of financial markets in many developed and developing countries have resulted in increased dis-intermediation and have made commercial banks vulnerable to interest rate risk. Relaxing exchange controls, adopting uniform accounting practices with regard to income recognition, assets classification and provisioning norms and prescribing capital adequacy norms has further aggravated the position. Now the developments in IT and telecommunications are allowing international pooling of financial resources thereby spreading the risk across more than one market.

He feels that Universal Banking System will come to stay in India in the near future. There is therefore need to prepare ourselves right now.

Sachdeva, (1987), [49] has made out a strong case for educating the bankers to take up preventive and detective measures. Frauds by some unscrupulous customers represent the problem of abuse of bank services. After elaborating the major forms of frauds in banks, he develops different preventive and detective techniques. The legal aspects of tackling the problem of frauds in banks are not however detailed by him. This is an important limitation of his study.

Sadare, (1984) [50] in his paper examined the issues in the measurement of productivity in commercial banks and stated that there is no positive co-relationship b/w manpower deployment and deposits, credit & business.

Sarker and Das, (1997), [51] compare performance of public, private and foreign banks for the year 1994-95 by using measures of profitability, productivity and financial management. They find PSBs comparing poorly with the other two categories. However, they caution that no firm inference can be derived from a comparison done for a single year.

Satyamurty, (1994), [52] clarified the concepts of profits, profitability & productivity applicable to the banking industry. It is organized by the bank managements that the pressure on the profitability is more due to the factors beyond their control. He suggested the technique of ratio analysis to evaluate the profit and profitability performance of banks. He opined that endeavors should be made to improve the spread performance through better funds management.

Saxena, (2000), [53] he analyzed the importance of IT in the banking sector. According to him, the future promises should be even more exciting, interesting and challenging. The Internet has enables us to talk to each customer as an individual, with different needs and requirements. This IT will affect the productivity and profitability of the banks.

Shah, (1977), [54] in his various papers discussed bank profitability and productivity. He expressed concern about increased expences and overheads. He favored written job descriptions for improvement of staff productivity. He also emphasized reduction of costs, creation of a team spirit, and improvement in the management for improving bank profitability and productivity.

Shah, (1986), [55] He attempted on empirical relationship between costs at branch level highlights the factors responsible for declining profitability and increasing operational cost at branch level. But the author could not find a feasible method for appropriating overhead cost to various services at the branch level.

Shanti, (1984), [56] has made a pioneering attempt to examine the issues relating to delivery of customer services in Indian banks as against the backdrop of a sound conceptual framework. She has provided an empirical analysis of bank employees job behavior and its relationship with bank services delivery. She has found that lack of job motivation, lack of freedom at branch level, lack of leadership qualities among bank managers, job security etc. have resulted in poor quality customer services in Indian banks.

Shapiro, (2000), [57] studied that the effects of cyberspace are evolving in ways that threaten privacy and other constitutional rights. It is eroding the liberty. The character of cyberspace is still up for grabs and different user environments yield widely different experiences. The nature of cyberspace may flip instead of promoting free and open exchange. It may end up controlling our lives in ways we have never imagined.

Shastri, (2000), [58] he analyzed the effect and challenges of new technology for banks. Technology has brought a sea-change in the functioning of the banks. The earlier manual system of preparation of vouchers, etc. is slowly being automated thereby saving a lot of time and effort. He emphasized on the use of ATMs and introduction of more ATMs than in the past, especially in the Post-VRS Scenario.

Singh, (1990), [59] he studies the productivity in the Indian Banking Industry. He studied Intra-bank, Inter-Bank groups and inter-bank groups productivity of public sector banks and SBI group. He analyzed branch productivity, per-employee productivity and financial parameters at constant prices. But his study did not considered nationalized Banks of 1980 and causes of varying productivity in banks.

Subrahmanyam, (1984), [60] in his paper discussed conceptual issue in productivity measurement and approach to interbank and inter temporal productivity comparisons. He highlighted some of the conceptual issue that is faced in the total factor productivity measurement associated with neutral technical progress.

Singhal's, (1987), [61] is yet another important study on customer services in Indian banks. This study is based on a research project of Sushila Singhal's, sponsored by Shri Ram Center for Industrial Relations., New Delhi. The study has two objectives: (a) "an adequate and systematic description analysis and explanation of customer services by the bank." This study is based on a broad sample of 528 bank employees (both officers and clerks) and 1,427 customers selected by a purpose-wise procedure. She had adopted a stage-wise methodology to select banks and in the second state five branches of the six banks for a more intensive study. The most important findings of this study are :

- There are considerable differences between different banks with regard to employees job involvement and motivation, customer loyalty and identification of banks and branches employees attitudes towards bank customers and colleagues, etc.

- The demographic and psychological variables were identified and their relationship with employee's job performance and customer service is explained.

- It is also found that there is no correlation between 'service efficiency' and 'customer satisfaction'; further she has also not found any systematic relationship between the size of bank branch and customer satisfaction. She also elaborately discussed the implications of her findings for efficient bank management. The important merit of her study is that it is based on multi-method and multi-variable approach to explain the bank employee's job behavior.

Swamy, (2001), [62] studied the comparative performance of different bank-groups since 1995-96 to 1999-2000. During this period, IT, new competition, deregulation took place. He studied three important aspects:

- What has been the impact of financial sector reforms on the structure of the Indian banking system?

- What are the advantages reaped by some of the new Indian private and foreign banks vis-à-vis PSBs?

- Whether new competition has enhanced the overall efficiency of the banking system?

In this study he made an attempt, in the context of financial sector reforms, to identify factors which could have led to changes in the position of individual banks in terms of their share in the overall banking industry. He analyzed the share of rural branches, average branch size, trends in bank's profitability, share of PSAs, share of wages in expenditure, provision and contingencies, net non performance assets in net advances, spread, has been calculated. He concludes that in many respects NPSBs are much better than PSBs, even they are better than foreign sector banks.

Thaur, (1987), [63] has brought out several interesting forms of abuse of bank services and facilities by customers in India. The non-repayment of loans, the submission of post-dated cheques by business for collection, raising overdraft from more than one bank; hypothecating the same inventory to more than one financial institution etc.

Tiku, (1986), [64] He studied the factors responsible for declining profitability over the years. The authors opined that there is a need to identify controllable and non-controllable factors both in income and costs so as to maintain a substantial spread between costs and they have identified the need for efforts from within banks in the form of cost control and from the government and monetary authorities in the form distinction between bank's commercial role and their social obligations.

Vageesh, (2000), [65] highly appreciated the NPSBs which have adopted IT. The NPSBs, with their state-of-the-art technology and grandiose plans to make in-roads into e-banking, are now darlings of the stock markets. Banks like HDFC & ICICI are foraying into net banking which offers great convenience to the customers on one hand and results in lower transaction costs for the banks on the other hand.

Vijay, K. & S.Annamalai, (2002), [66] they observed that human resources are considered to be the most valuable asset of any organization. It is essential to ensure that the human resource is utilized to a maximum level in order to realize the organizational goals. Their article deals with the crucial area of HRD/HRM under the head 'job satisfaction' and its significance in banking sector, factors associated with job satisfaction and dissatisfaction, present level of job satisfaction in different banking sectors etc. It also includes a measurement study conducted by the author and tries to provide some useful practical suggestions to improve the level of job satisfaction in banking sector in order to enhance the higher level of productivity. In this study out of 100 respondents in SBI and its associate banks only 25% of them have higher level of job satisfaction, 52% of them have medium level of job satisfaction and 23% of them have low level of job satisfaction. In nationalized banks out of 100 represents only 27% of them have higher level of job satisfaction 48% of them have medium level of job satisfaction and 25% of them have low level of job satisfaction. Also the study reveals out of 100 represents in private sector banks only 28% of them have high level of job satisfaction, 22% of them have medium level of job satisfaction and 50% of them have low level of job satisfaction. It could be observed from the study that the higher level of job satisfaction ratio is 25% in SBI and its associate banks, 27% in nationalized banks and 28% in private sector banks. Hence this study confirms that the level of job satisfaction ratio is higher in the private sector banks than nationalized banks and SBI and its associate banks.

Varde, (1979), [67] in his paper distinguished between effectiveness, efficiency and productivity and recommended that efficiency of a bank could be classified into four categories i.e. (i) manpower efficiency; (ii) operational efficiency; (iii) commercial efficiency; and (iv) efficiency of ancillary business. Efficiency according to each category can be measured separately, and measure of efficiency is productivity.

Venkatachalam, (1979), [68] highlighted the reasons for erosion in bank profits and profitability in recent years. The study is purely based on published figures. He argued that there is a trade-off between social obligations to be performed by the banks and increasing profits.

Verghese, (1983), [69] the work on profits and profitability of Indian commercial banks in the seventies is a comprehensive study on bank's profitability. It provides a useful analysis of the income statements of commercial banks during 1970-1979 but some concepts have limited applicability. For example, for the cost of usable funds the author used the absolute amount of establishment cost and otherwise expenses instead of proportionate amounts. But while calculating the net yield on advances the author has taken into account the cost of servicing of loans and advances.

Verma, (2000), [70] analyzed the impact of IT on PSBs and NPSBs in her article "Banking on Change'. The IT is a threat for the PSBs. It has to be a complete face off for the PSBs. With the business per employee, even for the front-run PSBs, a mere fraction of that of NPSBs, the PSBs have to do a lot on improving their productivity and efficiency. NPSBs are fully computerized and providing services on Internet. Especially ICICI bank, HDFC bank is very active on this front and is concentrating on Internet and e-commerce to offer their clientele a whole range of products under one roof. New banks like GTB, BOP, IDBI and UTI bank are not lagging behind. While some of them are concentrating on expansion and modernization, some are focusing on mergers and acquisitions for their growth.

Wadikar, (1980), [71] conducted a study of private sector banking in India since 1969. He discussed bank profitability in terms of assets and liability portfolio management and touched upon the trends in income and expenses of the private sector banks. The study revealed that performance of private sector scheduled commercial banks was better than public sector banks during 1969-76. The branch expansion was at a higher rate in private sector than in public sector banks and their spread in semi-urban and rural areas was also better.

Uppal R.K., (2000), [72] examines the impact of IT on the growth and performance of a cross- section of banks in India in his book. The study concentrates on 12 banks which have been categorized as follows-Group I three private sector banks which are fully computerized and providing services to customers on internet, Group II consists of three private banks fully computerized and not providing internet services, group III has three nationalized public sector banks and group IV has SBI and its associate banks. It offers various guidelines for the banking industry to improve its performance in the changed scenario characterized by openness, competition and prudence.

Zahir, (1980), [73] recommended transfer pricing as one of the important parameter for evaluating branch level performance of commercial banks. The determination of transfer price for branches should be based on the concept of opportunity cost. The application of the concept of transfer price mechanism for evaluating the branch level performance will give more meaning to profit statement of branches.

A review of the literature on the subject indicated that the introduction of BPR is very vital for the present banking system. The concept of BPR in its present form, is new, no comprehensive study has yet been made regarding the impact of BPR on banking industry. No doubt some articles in the leading newspapers, magazines and journals have highlighted the importance of BPR in banking industry.

1.5 Importance of the study

Banking in developing countries like ours has also started witnessing the changed technological and socio-economical factors, the emergence of new financial services has been provided with support of Information Technology, e.g. easy transfer of funds and messages across and beyond the national boundaries. Financial institutions, including banks, all over the world are, therefore, crucially dependent on products of IT and thus the need for BPR in banks.

Though the pace of change has been slow, yet the Indian banking scene is no exception to this phenomenon of transformation in products and services affected through IT. During the same period, i.e. the last decade, with the liberalization and opening up of Indian Economy, new private sector banks were established. Foreign banks also expanded their presence in India. The new private sector banks had a distinct advantage over the nationalized banks as they were able to start their operations with fully computerized services from day one. Foreign Banks were already offering such services.

The Nationalized Banks, with their social obligations, were having a large number of branches operating manually with a huge customer base. But then the presence of new private and foreign banks with their attractive products and service packages, the customers had several options. The products offered by these banks lured the customers away from the banks which did not offer them. This set a new trend in banking industry. Retaining the existing customer base and expanding the same became the order of the day. The competition among the banks became very intense.

The leading banks, therefore, quickly shifted their focus by re-engineering their processes to providing prompt, efficient customer service and offering variety of hi-tech banking products/services. In order to achieve the same, the leading nationalized banks started building up necessary infrastructure for introducing attractive hi-tech products and offering new services.

1.6 Research problem

From the various studies it is revealed that there is a mismatch between customer expectation and the services provided by the banks. The need to review and re-engineer their processes to withstand the competition as well as the growing needs of the economy, has almost made it mandatory for the commercial banks to reengineer their processes sooner or later. This gives rise to certain questions such as - What is the state of BPR in commercial banks. , What are the changes that have taken place, what is its impact on various factors such as growth, productivity, profitability, employees and customers? Are the banks really benefiting by re-engineering their processes etc.

The present study makes an attempt to answer some of these questions and understand the prevailing practices of BPR in commercial banks and explore the various factors relating the same. The study thus relates to "Business process Re- Engineering in Commercial Banks : A Case Study of State Bank of Hyderabad".

1.7 Research objectives of the study

The objectives of the study are to :

1. Examine the status of Business process Re- Engineering at SBH.
2. Study the impact of Business process Re- Engineering on performance of State Bank of Hyderabad.
3. Evaluate the impact of Business process Re- Engineering on Employees of State Bank of Hyderabad.
4. Find out the impact of Business process Re- Engineering on customer satisfaction in banks.

1.8 Hypotheses of the study

Based on the objectives set for the study the following hypotheses have been formulated

I. To Study the impact of Business process Re- Engineering on performance of State Bank of Hyderabad the following hypotheses are formulated.

Hypothesis 1

BPR at SBH is independent to the growth of SBH.

Hypothesis 2

BPR at SBH is independent to the employee and branch productivity of SBH.

Hypothesis 3

BPR at SBH is independent to the profitability of SBH.

II. To find out the impact of Business process Re-Engineering, on Employees of State Bank of Hyderabad. The following hypotheses are formulated.

Hypothesis 4

The awareness of the BPR initiatives among the employees of SBH is independent of the demographic variables of the respondent.

Hypothesis 5

The level of job satisfaction of the employees at SBH is independent of the demographic variables of the respondent.

Hypothesis 6

BPR and its impact on employees are independent of the demographic variables of the respondent.

Hypothesis 7

The overall impact of BPR at SBH is independent of the demographic variables of the respondent.

III. To evaluate the impact of Business process Re- Engineering on customer satisfaction in banks the following hypothesis are formulated.

Hypothesis 8

The frequency of visit by the respondents to the bank is independent of the demographic variables of the respondent.

Hypothesis 9

The customers' level of satisfaction of BPR at SBH is independent of the demographic variables of the respondent.

Hypothesis 10

The Customers perceptions about impact of BPR on stakeholders (customers, employees and bank), is independent of the demographic variables of the respondent.

1.9 Research Methodology

The details of research methodology adopted for the sample selection, data collection and data analysis of the present study are explained below :

1.10 Sample Design

The present study is based on both primary and secondary sources. Primary data is collected from sample customers and employees from sample branches of State Bank of Hyderabad. The sample employees are selected mainly from four major cities namely Hyderabad, Khammam, Warangal and Karimnagar. After the pilot survey it was found that all the employees in the bank are not aware of BPR in their banks and it was only branch manager and assistant manager were able to give information. Thereby 15 branches in each of these four cities were selected and the data was collected from both the assistant and branch managers along with 5 employees of BPR unit at SBH, thus the sample of employees constitute 125 in number (i.e. 4 × 15 × 2 + 5).

In selecting the sample customers 10 branches in Hyderabad were selected, and from each branch 25 customers were selected at random (10 × 25) i.e. 250 sample customers.

1.11 Methods of data collection

For the purpose of data collection from employees and customers, two different sets of structured questionnaires, the first set was served to the employees of selected branches of SBH to study the impact of Business Process reengineering in their banks. And the second set was used to collect the data from the customers of the selected branches, to study the impact of BPR on the customer satisfaction.

Apart from the questionnaire method, informal interviews and personal observations were also used to support and supplement the data generated through questionnaires.

The questionnaire which is executed to sample customers and employees covers various questions related to - 1) Objectives of BPR in banks (customers/employees perceptions of the same), 2) Awareness among the customers/employees of BPR initiatives taken up by the bank ,3) Level of satisfaction of the customers/employees with respect to BPR initiatives at SBH, 4) Impact of BPR on customers/employees,5) BPR's impact on bank's performance as perceived by customers/employees, 6) customers/Employees perceptions with regard to banking services before and after BPR, 7) Benefits of BPR to the customers/employees and 8) Problems faced by customers/employees due to BPR.

1.12 Analysis of data

The tools used for analysis in this study can be broadly classifies as (a) Descriptive and (b) Inferential. Statistical package for Social Sciences (SPSS) is used to generate necessary statistical tests.

(a) **Descriptive Analysis**

In descriptive analysis an attempt is made to explain the characteristic features of a particular variable. Simple statistical techniques like count, percentages, mean, weighted averages etc. have been used to analyze the data.

(b) **Inferential Analysis**

An inferential analysis for the purpose of this study has been carried out by, using ratios for testing the first three hypotheses and for the remaining hypotheses chi-square test was used.

1.13 Time frame

The time frame for the secondary data was the period from the financial year 2000 to 2009. Since BPR is implemented in SBH in the year 2004 the study period is 9 years, from the year 2000 to 2009 to study Pre BPR and Post BPR.

1.14 Limitations of the study

The primary data collected through questionnaire has its own limitations. Some of the sample customers and employees of the banks tend to exaggerate their problems whereas some others tend to underrate the actual figures pertaining to positive gains thereby distorting the actual facts and figures. Despite this, efforts were made to elicit correct information to the extent possible. While taking percentages or computing averages, numbers have been approximated thereby sometimes the total may not tally exactly.

The study has been confined to BPR in commercial banks with specific reference to State bank of Hyderabad. Thereby the sample respondents were restricted to only SBH branches. Every care has been taken to select the sample as representative of the universe. However, time and cost limitations will have their influence on the study.

1.15 Organization of the study

Keeping in view of the objectives, the study is organized into six chapters.

The first chapter, "Introduction" is devoted to make a brief presentation of Progress and trends of Indian banking sector. It also explains the rationale, objectives of the study, scope, methodology, limitations and the organization of the study.

The second chapter, 'Status of BPR at SBH' presents a detailed explanation on the subject of BPR and its various facets like importance , the different methodologies with special reference to BPR at SBH , along with the various BPR initiatives take up by SBH.

The third chapter ' Impact of BPR on performance of SBH' provides the description of ,the impact of BPR on growth , productivity and profitability of SBH from 2000 to 2009.The first phase of BPR was rolled out in the year 2004 in SBH, and so the year 2004 is taken as the base year and index is calculated prior BPR (i.e.2000 to 2003) and post BPR (i.e.2005 to 2009).Though we were aware of the impact on growth, profits and productivity of a bank is depending on many factors, efforts are made to study the same keeping in view the growth rate of GDP in Indian economy for the above period and the analysis is been done and conclusions made.

The fourth chapter 'Impact of BPR on employees of SBH – Analysis of Employees Perceptions', analyses the perceptions of 125 employees of state bank of Hyderabad of various branches to study the impact of BPR on its employees .The study includes analysis of employees perceptions, on objectives of BPR at SBH, awareness regarding the basic knowledge of BPR initiatives, benefits of BPR, level of satisfaction of employees with respect to BPR at their bank and also in the banking services provided by them after BPR, its impact on customers, employees and bank performance as perceived by employees, problems faced by the employees due to BPR in their bank if any.

The fifth chapter 'Impact of BPR on customers – Analysis of customer Perceptions' discusses the opinions of 250 SBH customers on various relevant issues on Business process Re-Engineering at SBH and its impact on the customer satisfaction. The issues examined include how customers perceive the objectives of BPR in banks, purpose of visiting the bank, frequency of visiting the bank, time taken for various transactions before and after BPR, awareness and usage of BPR services provided by banks, satisfaction about the banking services after BPR, benefits of BPR at SBH, problems faced by the customers after BPR in the bank, impact of BPR on customers, employees and bank performance.

The sixth chapter, 'Conclusions and Suggestions', discusses the conclusions that emerged from the analysis of the data during the study. Suggestions are also offered wherever necessary.

❖ ❖ ❖

CHAPTER - II

Status of BPR at SBH

2.1 Introduction

The traditional face of banks as mere financial intermediaries has altered because of the paradigm shift from balance-sheet to off-balance-sheet intermediation, from capital adequacy to capital efficiency and from banking to financial services. Appropriate risk management architecture is a function of size, complexity of business, risk philosophy, market perception and level of capital of banks. Competition needs to foster convergence towards best practices because of the growing role of market forces, the need for internationally consistent prudential norms, and the high-quality financial infrastructure.

Hence, risks need to be mitigated by improving integrated risk management mechanisms, streamlining systems and procedures and honing the skills of the operating staff. Enhanced organizational effectiveness of banks by deregulated interest management, judicious asset-liability management (ALM), realistic market segmentation, product differentiation, technology upgradation and corporate governance are needed for structural transformation

Improving efficiency and stability requires stress on reducing operating cost through higher techno-labour productivity, innovation and business process reengineering (BPR).Further there is a need for reduction in NPAs and greater fee-based business. Plans with respect to micro-planning, branch-centric profit planning, market-centric HRD policies and manpower planning are to be emphasized along with assimilation of core banking solution (CBS).

Measures relating, to customer-centricity, market focus, innovativeness, efficient credit dispensation and monitoring, besides building sound financials, can help banks overcome obstacles. To sustain profits, focus should be laid on declining spread, high operating costs, stiff competition, transformed economic environment and new prudential regulations. Technology needs to be integrated with business to raise the productivity bar significantly to foster innovation and strategic differentiation, higher value-added products and services with a competitive advantage.

2.2 Transformation of change in Indian Commercial Banks

The transformation of change in Indian commercial banks was seen during the post reform period i.e. based on Narsimham committee's recommendations. Commercial banks needed the transformation from laid back approach to fight back approach, from the era of socialism (all are equal) to an era of competition. The transformation of change in commercial banks is presented in table 2.1

Chart 2. 1

Transformation of change in Indian Commercial Banks

From	To
Inward Looking	Customer centric
Transaction Banking	Relationship Banking
Conservative bank for the older generation	Modern bank for the youth
Focus on branch administration	Focus on branch business
Slow, lumbering and bureaucratic	Aggressive, innovative and risk taking
Selling only banking products	Cross selling
Same salary and perks to all	Incentives and extra perks for good performers
Indifferent and arrogant staff	Energized friendly staff
What more the bank can give me	What I can give to the bank

SBI began addressing the technology gap that existed between it and its foreign-backed competitors. In the year 1990, SBI had to establish an automated teller network; when, it had not even automated its information systems. SBI responded by launching an ambitious technology drive, rolling out its own ATM network, then teaming up with GE Capital to issue its own credit card. In the early 2000s, the bank began cross-linking its banking network with its ATM network and Internet and telephone access, rolling out "anytime, anywhere" banking access. By 2002, the bank had succeeded in networking its 3,000 most profitable branches.

The implementation of new technology helped the bank achieve strong profit gains into the early years of the new century. SBI also adopted new human resources and retirement policies, helping trim its payroll by allowing its 20,000 employees, through voluntary retirement scheme.

By the beginning of 2004, SBI appeared to be well on its way to meeting the challenges offered by the deregulated Indian banking sector. The bank had become an aggressor into new territories, launching its own line of bancassurance products, and also initiating securities brokering services. In the meantime, SBI continued its technology rollout, boosting the number of networked branches to more than 4,000 at the end of 2003. SBI promised to remain a central figure in the Indian banking sector as it entered its third century.

State Bank of Hyderabad is the largest subsidiary bank of SBI which was constituted as Hyderabad State Bank on 8.8.1941 under Hyderabad State Bank Act, 1941. The Bank became a subsidiary of the State Bank of India on the 1st October 1959 and is now the largest Associate Bank of State Bank of India. Business Process Reengineering was launched in the year 2003 (consultants – Mckinsey) is one more step in the direction of revamping its processes to bring in world class capabilities in the organization and to respond to the 2C's, namely customer expectation and competitive pressure.

2.3 Business Process Re-engineering

BPR is the 'fundamental rethinking' and 'radical redesign' of business processes to bring about 'dramatic improvement' in performance.

Business Process Re-engineering (BPR) is the strategic analysis of business processes and the planning and implementation of improved business processes. The analysis is often customer centered and holistic in approach .BPR is a multi-disciplinary subject and should involve more than IT specialists. Nevertheless, IT can support BPR in many ways: Software can be used to help with gathering information about the current business organization. Workflow and process analysis tools, business modeling and simulation, On-line analytic processing (OLAP), Data mining all have a role to play.

Essentials of BPR

1. Clear vision of the future and specific goals for change,
2. Use of information technology,
3. Top management involvement,
4. Clear milestones and measurement, and
5. Training of the participants in process analysis and teamwork.

The key to reengineering is abandoning the most basic structural notions on which the modern organization is founded.

Importance of BPR

1. Increase in efficiency
2. Improves customer service

3. Reduces costs
4. Shares data and information
5. Use of Information Technology (IT): right place at right time
6. Reduces duplication, stove-pipe systems

Objectives of BPR

Business Process Redesign can be defined as -the analysis and design of workflow and processes within and between organizations- (Davenport & Short, 1990). BPR has three key target categories:

Customer Friendly : One of the main goals of introducing BPR is to get a competitive edge and that can only be gained by providing the customers more than what the others in the market are asking for.

Effectiveness : Providing product service effectively, ensures that the existing customers are retained and new customers are generated.

Efficiency : This is one of the key categories that are believed to be more important than any others. If a manufacturing company can master the skill of being efficient then they can automatically be more customers friendly and effective. Efficiency is not just about being efficient at the production floor level but the management level also has to be efficient.

Business Process Re-engineering is a management process used to re-define the mission statement, analyze the critical success factors, re-design the organizational structure and re-engineer the critical processes in order to improve customer satisfaction. BPR challenges managers to rethink their traditional methods of doing work and commit themselves to a customer-focused process. Many outstanding organizations have achieved and maintained their leadership through BPR [Oakland, 1995]. Companies using these techniques have reported significant bottom-line results, including better customer relations, reductions in cycle time to market, increased productivity, fewer defects/errors and increased profitability. BPR uses recognized techniques for improving business results and questions the effectiveness of the traditional organizational structure. Defining, measuring, analyzing and re-engineering work processes to improve customer satisfaction pays off in many different ways.

Business process is "a set of logically related tasks performed to achieve a defined business outcome."[1] A process is "a structured, measured set of activities designed to produce a specified output for a particular customer or market. It implies a strong emphasis on how work is done within an organization"[2]

Processes have two important characteristics

They have customers (internal or external), (ii) They posses cross-organizational boundaries, i.e., they occur across or between organizational subunits. One technique for identifying business processes in an organization is the value chain method [3].

Processes are generally identified in terms of beginning and ends, interfaces, and organization units involved, particularly the customer unit. High Impact processes should have process owners. Examples of processes include developing a new product; ordering goods from a supplier; creating marketing plan; processing and paying an insurance claim, etc

Processes can be based on three dimensions

Entities : Processes take place between organizational entities. They could be Inter-organizational (e.g. EDI, i.e., Electronic Data Interchange), Interventional or Interpersonal (e.g. CSCW, i.e., Computer Supported Cooperative Work).

Objects : Processes result in manipulation of objects. These objects could be Physical or Informational.

Activities : Processes could involve two types of activities: Managerial (e.g. develop a budget) and Operational (e.g. fill a customer order).

The concept of Re-engineering traces its origins back to management theories developed as early as the nineteenth century. The purpose of Re-engineering is to "make all the processes the best-in-class".

The traditional approach considers that managers could discover the best processes for performing work and reengineer them to optimize productivity[5]. BPR echoes the classical belief that there is one best way to conduct tasks. In Taylor's time, technology did not allow large companies to design processes in a cross-functional or cross-departmental manner. Specialization was the state-of-the-art method to improve efficiency given the technology of the time.

In the early 1900's, the concept of Re-engineering is "To conduct the undertaking toward its objectives by seeking to derive optimum advantage from all available resources"[6]. Although the technological resources of our era have changed, the concept still holds."It is not enough to hold

People accountable for certain activities, it is also essential to delegate to them the necessary authority to discharge that responsibility."[7].

It was considered that classical organization theory is obsolete, classical ideas such as division of labor has had an enduring power and applicability that Re-engineering has so far failed to demonstrate. BPR does not appear to qualify as a scientific theory, because, among other things, it is not duplicable and it has limited scope. The applicability of classical management theories, such as division of labor, was widely duplicable and portable. These ideas stimulated increases in productivity, output, and income that led to the creation of the middle class.[8]

It was pointed out that conflict is often a driving force in organizational behavior. BPR claims to stress teamwork, yet paradoxically, it must be "driven" by a leader who is prepared to be ruthless. One executive with BPR experience warns not to assume "you can simply issue directives from the center and expect it to happen."[9]

Classical Re-engineering, repeats the same mistakes as the classical approach to management by separating the design of work from its execution. Typically, a small Re-engineering team, often from outside the company, designs work for the many. [10]

Thus BPR is defined as a systematic approach or methodology for analyzing business activities or processes with a view to achieve these objectives, improving the organization's alignment with strategic goals and its effectiveness, efficiency, competitiveness.

2.4 BPR Methodologies

Based on different sources there are four methodologies :

Table - 2.2

Selected Business Re-engineering Methodologies

Source	Methodology
Academics	Davenport and Short
Consultants (Academic Background)	Hammer/Champy
Consultants	Manganelli/Klein
Users	Kodak

2.5 Davenport and Short (1990)

He prescribes a five-step approach to BPR namely to develop the Business Vision and Process Objectives: BPR is driven by a business vision, which implies specific business objectives such as Cost Reduction, Time Reduction, Output Quality improvement, QWL (Quality of Work Life) /Learning/Empowerment. (cf: Shared Vision of Senge 1990, Ikujiro & Nonaka 1995).

Identify the Processes to be redesigned: Most firms use the High- Impact approach, which focuses on the most important processes or those, which conflict most with the business vision. Lesser number of firms uses the Exhaustive approach that attempts to identify all the processes within an organization and then prioritize them in order of redesign urgency.

Understand and Measure the Existing Processes: For avoiding the repeating of old mistakes and for providing a baseline for future improvements.

Identify IT Levers : Awareness of IT capabilities can and should influence process design.

Design and Build a Prototype of the New Process : The actual design should not be viewed as the end of the BPR process. Rather, it should be viewed as a prototype, with successive iterations. The metaphor of prototype aligns the BPR approach with quick delivery of results, and the involvement and satisfaction of customers.

2.6 The Hammer/Champy Methodology

Hammer/Champy popularized Business Re-engineering. Hammer, a former M.I.T. professor turned into a consultant, and Champy, president of the worldwide consulting company CSC Index, define Business Re-engineering as a fundamental rethinking and radical redesign of mission critical business processes (Hammer/ Champy, 1993). Hammer/Champy sees poor management and unclear objectives as the main problems to Business Re-engineering success. Only just recently, they acknowledge people's resistance as a major obstacle to Business Re-engineering successful implementation (Davenport, 1996). Their Business Re-engineering methodology, which was fine-tuned by Champy's consulting company, breaks into six steps namely –

Introduction into Business Re-engineering : The CEO initiates the project. She describes briefly and pragmatically the current business situation to start actions. She introduces her vision to the employees of the company

Identification of Business Processes : This step looks at the broad picture, of how processes interact within the company and in relation to the outside world. One deliverable is a graphical display of all processes

Selection of Business Processes : The third step serves to select such processes, which - once reengineered - will lead to high value for the company's customers. In addition, processes that lend themselves to easy Re-engineering are being selected.

Understanding the Selected Business Processes : This step does not dwell on a detailed analysis of the functioning of the selected business processes, rather concentrates on the performance of the current processes as opposed to what is expected from them in the future.

Redesign of the Selected Business Processes : The fifth step is according to Hammer/Champy the most creative of all. Imagination, lateral thinking and some sort of craziness characterize it.

Implementation of Redesigned Business Processes : The last step covers the implementation phase of the Business Re-engineering project. Hammer/Champy does not talk about implementation as much as about project planning. They believe in the success of the implementation, once the five preliminary steps have been properly performed

2.7 The Davenport Methodology

Davenport puts Information Technology at the heart of Business Re-engineering. For Davenport Information Technology possesses the most important role for innovating Business Processes. Despite his emphasis on innovation and technology, Davenport states, that organizational and human resource issues are more central, than technology issues to the behavior issues that must occur to within a business process. Davenport sees culture as a constraint, when there is a poor process innovation to cultural fit. With regard to managing the change, Davenport emphasizes traditional management functions, like planning, directing, monitoring, decision-making and communicating (Davenport/Short, 1990 and Davenport, 1993).

Davenport is convinced, that Business Re-engineering should better integrate with the other non-revolutionary (incremental) process approaches, like Total Quality Management (Davenport, 1996). His methodology covers six steps -

- **Visioning and Goal setting :** The first step is needed to focus all subsequent actions on company visions and process goals. Cost reduction is considered an important goal, yet Davenport warns against concentrating too much on cost cutting, because other goals, such as worker satisfaction, reduction of time requirements, and improvement of process performance might be discriminated against.

Identification of Business Processes : This step identifies the business processes, which should be reengineered. Davenport advises Business Re-engineering teams to concentrate on a few important, not more than 15 core processes.

Understand and Measure Processes : The third step studies the exact functioning and performance of the selected Business Processes. This differentiates Davenport from the Hammer/Champy approach. Davenport in particular wants to make sure, that during the process redesign old practices are not being "reinvented" and performance benchmarks for the redesigned processes are being set up.

Information Technology : The fourth step serves to study the applicability of Information Technology tools and applications for the newly designed work processes.

Process prototype : This step covers the design of a functioning prototype of the new Business Process. People in the company study this prototype, develop ideas for enhancements and make themselves comfortable with the redesign of their work processes.

Implementation : The last step serves to implement the tested prototype on a company-wide basis. Davenport considers this step crucial to the success of the overall effort, since implementation takes roughly double as long (minimum one year) as the foregoing steps.

2.8 The Manganelli/Klein Methodology

Manganelli/Klein argues, to only concentrate on those Business Processes that directly support the strategic goals of the company and customer requirements. Product development (a knowledge process) is such a preferred Business Process. The see organizational impact, time, risk, and cost as obstacles to success. They claim, Business Re-engineering to be more successful than incremental change initiatives, which tend to fail more often (Manganelli/Klein, 1994). The Manganelli/Klein Business Re-engineering methodology Rapid-Re (tm), which is supplemented by the Rapid-Re Re-engineering Software toolset for Microsoft Windows (tm), breaks into five steps-

Preparation : The first step asks all directly involved persons to define goals and to prepare for the Business Re-engineering project.

Identification : This step defines a customer oriented process model of the organization, as well as selects key business processes for redesign.

Vision : The third step serves to define at which performance level the process currently delivers, and which higher level is required for the future.

Re-Design : This step breaks into two parallel sub-steps The Technical Design deals with Information Technology Design to support the new processes. The Social Design step serves to design new work environments for the people, including organizational and personnel development plans.

Transformation : The fifth step is meant to implement the redesigned processes and work environments within the organization.

2.9 The Kodak Methodology

The international Kodak organization developed a Business Re-engineering methodology that is being applied to Kodak facilities around the world. Similar to other practitioner approaches, has the Kodak methodology been influenced by Hammer/Champy. The Kodak methodology breaks into five steps :

Project Initiation : The first step is considered key. It covers project planning and definition of all project administration rules and procedures.

Process Understanding : This step sets the project team up, designs a comprehensive process model for the organization and assigns process managers, who will be responsible for the redesigned process after implementation.

New Process Design : The third step covers the redesign of selected Business Processes, taking into account the potentials of Information Technology. This step ends with the planning of a Pilot Implementation of the redesigned processes.

Business Transition : The fourth step is focused towards the implementation of the newly designed processes within the organization. Part of this step is the adaptation of the organization's infrastructure to the requirements of the newly designed processes.

Change Management : The last step is being performed parallel to the first four steps. The project team handles barriers, which crop up during the course of the Business Re-engineering project.

2.10 Role of Information Technology in Banking

Banking all over the world during last decade witnessed changes which perhaps it did not see during its entire history. The changes are not only confined to developed countries. Banking in developing countries like ours has started witnessing these changes. The changed technological and socio-economical factors, the emergence of new financial services has been provided with support of Information Technology, e.g. easy transfer of funds and messages across and beyond the national boundaries. Financial institutions, including banks, all over the world are, therefore, crucially dependent on products of IT and thus the need for BPR in banks.

Though the pace of change has been slow, yet the Indian banking scene is no exception to this phenomenon of transformation in products and services affected through IT. During the same period, i.e. the last decade, with the liberalization and opening up of Indian Economy, new private sector banks were established. Foreign banks also expanded their presence in India. The new private sector banks had a distinct advantage over the nationalized banks as they were able to start their operations with fully computerized services from day one. Foreign Banks were already offering such services.

The Nationalized Banks, with their social obligations, were having a large number of branches operating manually and a huge customer base. But then the presence of new private and foreign banks with their attractive products and service packages, the customers had several options. The products offered by these banks lured the customers away from the banks which did not offer them. This set a new trend in banking industry. Retaining the existing customer base and expanding the same became the order of the day. The competition among the banks became very intense

The leading banks, therefore, quickly shifted their focus by re-engineering their processes to providing prompt, efficient customer service and offering variety of hi-tech banking products/services. In order to achieve the same, the leading nationalized banks started building up necessary infrastructure for introducing attractive hi-tech products and offering new services.

For, service sector sustaining long-term customer relationship management (CRM) has become a challenge with almost everyone in the market with similar products. With productivity, efficiency and profitability gaining currency as a 'mantra' for banks in the present day context, the pricing of products, be it deposit or advance has become more complex. IT comes to the rescue of banking sector.

As the Basel II Capital Accord continues to evolve it requires banks to implement a comprehensive risk framework across the institution. One of the key challenges which the banks are facing in the implementation of the Basel II is the Assimilation of new processes and reengineering of existing processes.

Information Technology has basically been used under two different avenues in Banking. One is Communication and Connectivity and other is Business Process Reengineering. Information technology enables sophisticated product development, better market infrastructure, implementation of reliable techniques for control of risks and helps the financial intermediaries to reach geographically distant and diversified markets.

2.11 Business Process Re-engineering at State Bank of Hyderabad

State Bank of Hyderabad is a subsidiary of the State Bank of India and is currently the largest Associate Bank of State Bank of India. State Bank of Hyderabad was constituted as Hyderabad State Bank on 8.8.1941 under Hyderabad State Bank Act, 1941. The first branch of the Bank was opened at Gunfoundry, Hyderabad on 5th April, 1942.

State Bank of Hyderabad had the unique distinction of being the central bank of the erstwhile State of Hyderabad, covering present-day Telangana region of Andhra Pradesh, Hyderabad-Karnataka of Karnataka and Marathwada of Maharashtra, to manage its currency - Osmania Sikka and public debt apart from the functions of commercial banking.

In 1953, State Bank of Hyderabad took over the assets and liabilities of the Hyderabad Mercantile Bank Ltd. In 1956, the Bank was taken over by Reserve Bank of India as its first subsidiary and its name was changed from Hyderabad State Bank to State Bank of Hyderabad. In 1959, State Bank of Hyderabad became a subsidiary of the State Bank of India.

The objective of BPR initiative is to strengthen Bank's ability to acquire new customers, build lasting relationships with existing customers and increase customer satisfaction through world-class service quality. The BPR project is also to simplify and redesign business processes to fully leverage the Core Banking Solution (CBS) platform.

CBS and BPR together will lead to creation of a new sales and service platform across the metro and urban branch network. The aim is to improve Bank's performance in key business areas.

The re-engineering of business processes at State Bank of Hyderabad started mainly because there was a mismatch between customer expectations and the bank process capabilities. The other reasons for implementing BPR at the bank is due to

1. Intense competition from other banks
2. Increasing customer expectations
3. Change from old business practices.

2.12 Objectives of BPR at SBH

The objectives of BPR at SBH is to -

1. Simplify customer facing branch processes.
2. Migrate non-customer facing processes to central processing centers.
3. Empower branches to become sales, service and marketing units.
4. Raise customer satisfaction levels
5. To enhance productivity.

The year 2004 was the designing phase for BPR at SBh. During the year, the BPR Project has successfully implemented its first phase of roll out. Non-CBS dependant initiatives were rolled out across all the Circles for reduction in turnaround time for sanction of loans, skill pooling and to improve quality of appraisal & sanction. Retail Assets Central Processing Centres (RACPCs) and Small Enterprises Credit Cells (SECCs) were created in 14 major cities, covering all the Circles. For improving quality of service to the customers, initiatives like Grahak Mitra and Drop Box were launched. To provide a superior Banking experience for the high net-worth customers, Relationship Manager (PB) concept has been implemented. To migrate customers to Alternate Channel of service delivery, a highly successful initiative by way of ATM migration was launched. Currency Administration Cells are set up to manage idle cash at Branches and to eliminate the drudgery for the Branch staff in transporting currency. All these initiatives have resulted in significant improvement in customer service levels, reduction in operating costs for the Bank and creation of highly skilled and motivated BPR Implementation Teams.

2.13 Need for BPR at SBH

1. To improve customer service at branch, so as to enable to meet Competition.
2. To meet Customer expectations and timely delivery of products.
3. To improve relationship building.
4. To enable branches to focus on marketing and customer service.
5. To enable Bank to redeploy and pool skilled man power to meet Corporate concerns (Asset quality and Non performance Assets Recovery).
6. Reduce Process related work at branches by shifting the same to back office processing centre.
7. Shift repetitive activities to back office processing centers.

2.14 List of activities of SBH with the BPR outfit

The various services at SBH along with BPR initiatives are presented in the table below :

Table 2.3

Activity n the Branch	BPR Outfit
Cash transactions, customer rush	ATM, Drop Box
Customer service in the branch	Grahak mitra
Customer Relationship building	Relationship Manager.
Central Govt. Pensions	Pension Processing Cell
Advances – appraisal / sanctions / follow up / recovery	Loan Processing Centres. (Retail and MSME)
Recovery of NPA, sick/sticky loan accounts.	Stressed Assets Resolution Centres
Bank Guarantees, Letter of Credits, Bills, Forex Related transactions	Trade Finance Centralized Processing Centre.
Deposit account opening, maintenance, cheque book issue.	Liability Centralized Processing Centre.
Cash Management	Currency Administration Cells

List of activities of SBH with the BPR outfit

List of activities of SBH with the BPR outfit banking industry is undergoing rapid and radical changes driven by technology, innovation in products and services and ever expanding customer expectations. To address such challenges effectively, the Bank rolled out the following BPR initiatives that create value and quality for the customers. BPR at SBH branches are focused on customer service and sales. They can be categorized under four heads and considered as four pillars of BPR at SBH.

2.15 Four Pillars of BPR at SBH

1. Customer facing initiatives.(Sales Forces)
2. Non-customer facing initiatives.(CPC's)
3. Alternate Delivery channels.
4. Branch redesign. (New branch format)

Customer facing initiatives is also known as front end initiatives and non- customer facing initiatives are considered as back end initiatives.

The various products under these initiatives can be clearly understood by the following chart 2.4

Chart 2.4

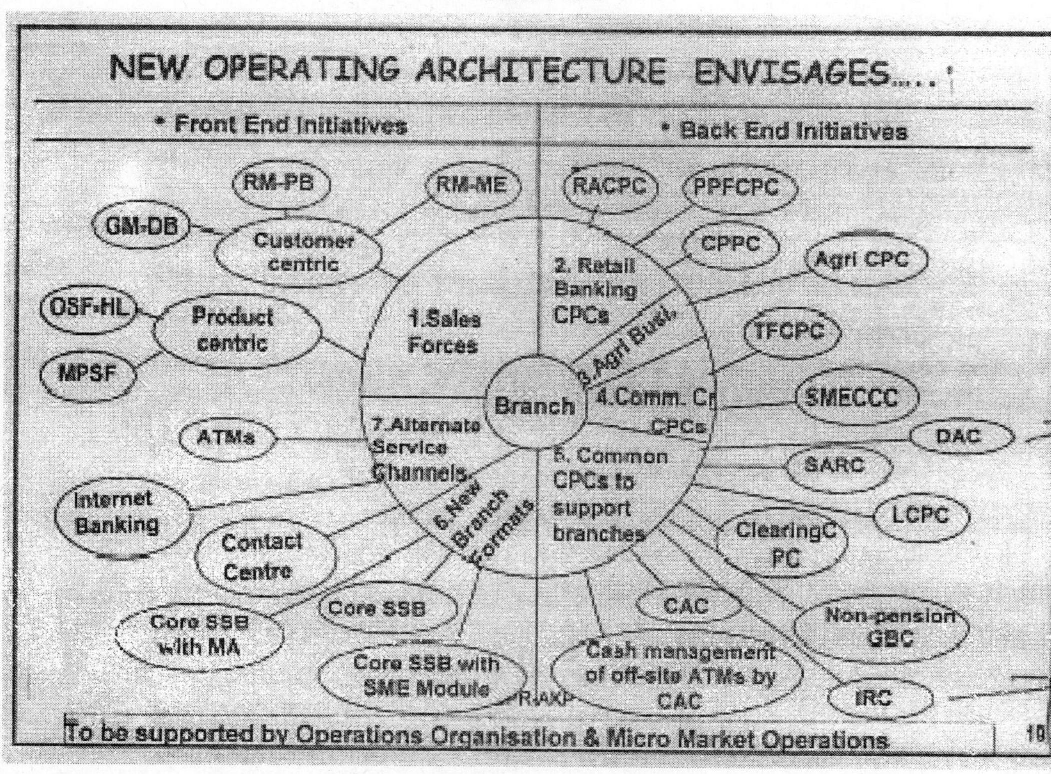

The architecture of Business Process Re-Engineering in State Bank of Hyderabad

The various BPR initiatives at SBH is explained below :

Customer facing initiatives. (Sales Force) – SBH is trying to build relationships by meeting the needs of customers through -

Grahak Mitras – Here the customer feels welcomed and assisted by an assistant positioned in the customer area to greet and guide the walk – in – customers. And he also assist the customers in using alternate delivery channels like ATM, Internet banking, RTGS, NEFT etc. This initiative has been implemented in 145 centres covering 430 branches. The bench mark fixed by SBH for ATM applications is 20 per day, Migration to drop box 100% and internet applications 5 per day.

Drop Boxes – To expedite and facilitate easier Cheque tendering, the Bank has provided specially designed drop boxes at 204 centres covering 680 branches. These boxes enhance customer convenience of depositing local clearing and out station cheques. It eliminates customer waiting time and frees the branch personnel from receipt of clearing and collection of cheques.

Relationship Manager (PB) – They gain, maintain, retain and grow relationships. They offer relationship banking facility to high net worth customers and thus maximize value per account by cross selling and up selling , resulting in addition of new high value customers.

Relationship Manager (ME) – They develop product relationship with existing customers. They prepare and process medium enterprise proposals. They identify potential ME customers in the area and form strategies to acquire them. Address customers promptly and monitor portfolio accounts for early warning. To offer exclusive personalized services to high end customers of both PER and ME segments, Relationship Managers have been posted at 106 Branches (RM-PB: 64 branches at 32 centres & RM-ME: 42 branches covering 7 centres).

Sales Forces - To avail the benefit of having specialized loan processing centres are manned by skilled staff at smaller centres having less than 10 branches, Mini CPCs have been launched at Karimnagar, Gulbarga, Khammam, Nizamabad, Nanded, Ramagundem, Mahoobnagar, Guntur and Kakinada centres. There are three major Loan Processing Centers- namely 1) Home loan sales team (HLST),2) Multi-product sales team for retail and SME products{MPST},(excluding home loans)and 3) combined sales team (CST) – all types of products at smaller centers. For giving thrust to increase the Bank's market share, Marketing teams (OSF-HL, MPSF & CSF) specially designed to mobilize and market P segment and Small Enterprises segment assets and liability products have been established at 9 centres viz. Hyderabad, Vizag, New Delhi, Chennai, Bangalore, Mumbai, Aurangabad, Vijaywada and Warangal.

Non-customer facing initiatives role is to shorten TAT

Retail Assets CPC (RACPC) – It looks into the appraisal, sanction, disbursement, maintenance and recovery of retail loans. RACPC; Two Retail Assets Central Processing Centre are functioning at Hyderabad & Secunderabad (covering all Twin City branches) Products Handled at these centers are: Housing Loan, Mortgage Loan, Car Loan, Educational Loan).To further improve the service and give single point credit delivery system, RACPC-Hyderabad has been converted to a fully computerized End State RACPC on CBS platform. 89 branches of Hyderabad are linked to the centre. Besides speedy appraisal, sanction & documentation of housing, education, vehicle and mortgage loans, all other processes including account maintenance, set up, supervision and monitoring is done through skilled personnel.

SME credit centre (SMECC) – It ensures appraisal, sanction, disbursement, maintenance and recovery of SE loans and maintenance of ME loans. Small Enterprises Credit Cells (SECC) at Hyderabad has also been converted to a fully computerized End State SMECCC on CBS platform. 81 branches of Hyderabad are linked to the centre. All credit requirements of SME borrowers are being processed at the centre thereby making it a single point delivery system. SMECCC: Small and Medium Enterprises City Credit Centre: Has 95 branches Covering Micro, Small and Medium Enterprises I C&l units (Industries and Business units with an actual turnover upto Rs. 25 Crores). "Micro Marketing Study" initiative was launched at Hyderabad Centre to conduct an in-depth market survey of the twin cities of Hyderabad and Secunderabad. The study focuses on re-designing the Branch network so that the right type of Branches at the right location with appropriate staffing can be established to exploit the full potential of the market.

RASECC/RASMECCC - RASECCs (Combined cells for processing Retail & Small Enterprises loan proposals) at Aurangabad, Vizag, Vijaywada and Warangal centers have o been converted to fully computerized End State RASMECC on CBS platform. The remaining four centres at Chennai, Mumbai, New Delhi and Bangalore will be taken up for conversion to End State RASMECC during the next financial year. RASMECCC:Retáil Asssets and Small and Medium Enterprises City Credit Centre are functioning at 8 centres covering 129 branches.

Agri CPC - It sees to the appraisal, sanction, documentation of Agri loans. The Agri-CPC was launched at Karimnagar,Parbhani and Nizamabad Centres designed to source, market, process and sanction agricultural loans (ACC/KCC/ATL) at intensive agricultural centres thereby, providing efficient service to the farmers.

Currency Administration Cell (CAC) – It determines and distributes optimal cash balance at the branches. To improve the efficiency of cash management, Currency

Administration Cells (CACs) have been opened at 11 centres linking 155 branches. The average cash holding of the linked branches has been reduced by 60%. Replenishment of cash at OFF-SITE ATMs by CAC is an initiative that has been operationalised at Aurangabad and is proposed to be extended to off-site ATMs at Hyderabad in the next phase.

Liability CPC – Opening/closing of deposit accounts and supply of welcome kit is processed at this center. It also looks into Centralized Processing of Inward and Outward Clearing Instruments. 'The Core Banking Platform and online connectivity to all the branches is leveraged for this activity. Thus the repetitive activity of cheque handling is shifted from branches.

Clearing CPC – Performs all clearing related activities (inward and outward) and also service branch functions. Centralized pension processing cell (Pension CPC) – Processes all central government pensions and credits directly to their customers account. Centralized Pension Processing Centre (CPPC) was established at Secunderabad for ensuring smooth and efficient processing of Central Government pensions. The cell is processing 36,668 pension payment orders of central government pensioners pertaining to 696 branches. As on March 2008, 19,995 pensioners pertaining to 425 branches are being paid their pensions online through CPPC. Centralized calculations of Central Government Pensions of pensioners having accounts with the branches are carried on at this centre. That is Centralized payment of pensions on a monthly basis to all Central Government pensioners (around 40000) of 753 branches of SBH. Calculation and payment of arrears to various categories of pensioners is done through this Centralized Processing Centre.

Trade finance CPC (TFCPC) – It works with trade related transactions both in foreign currency and local currency. Trade Finance Central Processing Centre (TFCPC) was launched at Hyderabad in January 2008 to handle all business related to Trade Finance like LCs, Bills, Guarantees (both Inland and Foreign) centrally. Seven forex intensive branches have been linked to the centre during the current financial year. The remaining branches of the city will be linked to TFCPC during financial year 2008-09.

Stressed assets resolution centre - Stressed Assets Resolution Centre (SARC) initiative was launched at Hyderabad centre specifically to recover and manage hardcore NPAs, thereby allowing the Branches to focus on new business while converting their NPAs into productive assets with least time & cost. 65 branches of Hyderabad city have been linked to the centre. The main objectives and activities of SARC I Hybrid SARC are :

1. To own stressed assets of MSMEIC&l and PER segment accounts. (Staff and AGR segment accounts are not covered by SARC/Hybrid SARC.)

2. To draw account wise strategy for recovery of bank dues.
3. To arrange for Rehabilitation & Restructuring of viable stressed assets
4. To explore and handle compromise settlements including 0 T S, Lok Adalats and Bank adalats.
5. Where compromises are not forth coming despite best efforts initiation of legal process by filing of suits, initiation of action under SARFAESI Act, 2002.
6. Follow up of AUC accounts where suits are not filed, seeking approvals of appropriate authorities for reversal of entries in AUC accounts if no recoveries are forthcoming.
7. To recommend for write offs in deserving cases where prospects for recovery are very bleak.
8. Initiation of legal action for cheques bounced u/s 138 of N I Act.

2.18 The activities undertaken by CPC's are listed in the chart2.5 below :

Chart 2.5

Activity chart of CPC's

ACTIVITY	**Linked to any Loan Processing centre**	**Each linked to Mini CPC or Rural CPC (80 Branches)**	**Branches linked to End- state loan CPCs. (227 branches)**
Marketing, Sourcing the application. KYC compliance Maintain relationship with customer.	Branch	Branch	Branch/Sales Teams
Pro sanction Inspection, KYC verification, appraisal of proposal, sanction.	Branch	Mini/Rural CPC	Loan CPC
Documentation, Disbursal, post sanction inspection, periodic inspections, follow up for recovery.	Branch	Branch	Loan CPC
Non Performance Assets Recovery/compromise/ write off! suit filing etc.	Branch	Branch	Stressed Assets Resolution Centre.

2.19 Non customer facing initiatives CPC's - objective

Is to ensure quality of assets and reduce the turnaround time. It involves -

1. Skill pools – team of people focusing on same job repeatedly thus attaining specialization.
2. Standardization of processes – same system being followed across the bank leaving less room for interpretation.
3. Automation – use of technology to eliminate human error.

2.20 Benefits of non customer facing initiatives

1. Enables to minimize the time of transaction banking by reducing the work of the staff.
2. Saves time on acceptance of clearing / collection instruments from customers.
3. Outward clearing instruments are processed by CPC.
4. Enables sorting at CPC, as sorting is done through automated machines, resulting in saving time and man hours.
5. Proceeds of outward clearing instruments are afforded directly by clearing CPC.
6. All inward clearing instruments will be retained by clearing CPC and concerned accounts will be directly debited, thereby reducing the branch workload.
7. By just filling a few mandatory fields, deposit accounts can be opened in quick time in the presence of the customer. Remaining back office updations will be done by liability CPC.
8. Welcome kit and personalized cheque books will be provided by liability CPC.
9. Currency administration cell helps in maintaining hand balance at branches relieving branches from cash remittance work.
10. Pension CPC will calculate and credit central govt. pensions directly.
11. Loan related work of most of the personal segment loans like housing, car, education, SME and agriculture will be carried out by respective CPC's.

Alternate Delivery channels

ATM's - SBH's ATM Debit card services offer customers easy access to money anytime from anywhere. The card is safe and secure and eliminates the need to carry large amounts of cash. It saves time and the inconvenience of going to the bank for cash withdrawals. Withdrawing facility can be obtained from Savings and Current accounts, including overdraft accounts. It enables the customers to view the current balance and also a mini statement of the last five transactions on your account. SBH e provides a Personal Identification Number (PIN) while receiving the card. ATM cum Debit Cards issued by the Bank can be used at more than 12500 ATMs of Andhra Bank, Bank of India, Corporation Bank, Dena Bank, HDFC Bank, Indian Bank, IndusInd Bank, Punjab National Bank, UCO Bank, Union Bank of India , UTI Bank, Canara Bank and Bank of Rajasthan which are members of bilateral sharing arrangement. Charges for such usage are as under w.e.f 01.04.2008

Chart 2.6

Revised Service Charges at ATM's

Transaction Type	Revised Rate per Transaction (Rs.)
Cash withdrawal	20.00
Balance enquiry	NIL

ATM cum Debit Cards issued by the Bank can also be used in India at the ATMs ,other than those under bilateral sharing arrangement, displaying any one or all of MasterCard, Maestro or Cirrus Logos. The Bank's International Debit Card can be used at more than 10, 00,000 ATMs across the world, displaying any one or all of MasterCard, Maestro or Cirrus Logos. The rates for such usage have been revised with effect from 01.10.2006. Revised charges are as under –

Chart 2.7

Revised Service Charges for using other than SBH ATM's

Service	Revised Charges
Our Cardholders using State Bank Group ATMs for any Purpose	NIL
Our Cardholders using Other Bank ATMs for BALANCE ENQUIRY	Free
Our Cardholders using Other Bank ATMs for CASH WITHDRAWAL	Rs. 20/- Per Transaction all inclusive and no other charges will be levied to the customer with effect from 01.04.2008

Internet banking - State Bank of Hyderabad online banking is available to all customers of the bank. State Bank of Hyderabad net banking requires the user to have a User Id and Password. SBH online banking is possible through any computer or equivalent function hand held device connected to the World Wide Web.

Online Transactions : State Bank of Hyderabad Internet banking is possible only through the dedicated website provided by the bank. The customer may undertake the following banking related transactions :

1. Download and print the bank account statement
2. Order new cheque books by email.
3. Modify his or her email address
4. Modify the banking password
5. Demand draft may be ordered online
6. Check the status of Current bank account and Savings bank account.
7. Inquire online on the status of encashment of cheque

Contact centers

Branch redesign (New branch format)

By supporting the branches with various processing and back office centers, the branches to be redesigned as per BPR redesign model with the following specifications

1. A branch to have 60-70% of space for customers and the remaining for branch staff.
2. A customer friendly ambience and specific demarcation of functional lobbies to be created in branches.
3. The branch to have three clearly demarcated areas/lobbies.

   Self Service Lobby : Where Grahak Mitra, Internet kiosk and various broachers of bank products are kept

   Service Lobby : It is the transaction zone where Service Manager and Single Window operator attend to customer requirements.

   Sales Lobby : where the asset and liability products of the Bank are sold to customers by Relationship Managers.

4. A Customer Relation Officer will be identified for each branch. A CR0 fulfills the role of customer relationship, Welcome Kit handling, and product selling at the branch.

A redesigned branch layout in presented in chart 2.8

Chart 2.8

Redesigned Branch Layout

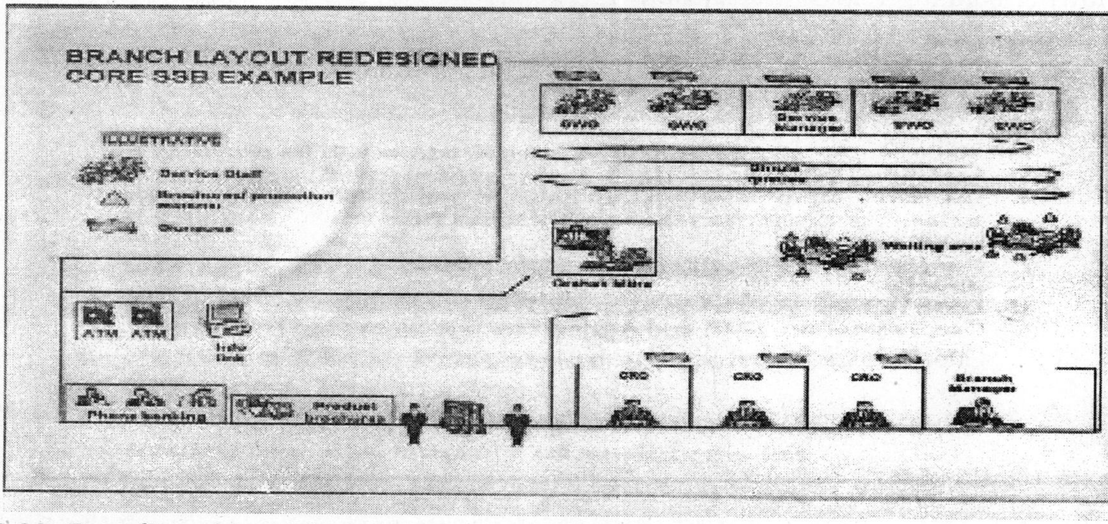

2.23 Benefits of branch redesign

1. More customer area, in the branch.
2. Reduction in customer waiting time, in the branch.
3. Alternate channels including drop boxes enables the customers to perform basic transactions and provide information 24 x 7.
4. Customer service officer and SWO will be a single point for service to customers.
5. Branch managers can focus on sales rather than routine branch management.

2.24 Future Plan of Action of BPR at SBH

300 Metro I Urban I Semi Urban Branches are now linked to various BPR initiatives (Processing Centers)

1. All Branches to be linked to Liability Processing Centre during this year
2. 7 More Loan Processing Centres, Two more Cash Administration Cells and one Cash Administration Branch will be launched during this current year.
3. 40-50% of branches will be under BPR by the end of this year

2.25 Working of CPCs -

a. **Opening of a new account is one of the key tasks of a CRO.** The customer enters the branch and meets the Grahak Mitra who welcomes him to the branch and enquires on the purpose of his visit. The Grahak.Mitra then hands over an application form for deposit account to the customers and tells him about the documents which are required for address and identity proof for opening the account. In case the customer has brought along the relevant documents with him, the Grahak Mitra will help him fill in the application form and provide him with a token. The customer will then be directed to a separate seating area in front of the CROs.

b. **One of the CROs will call the customer when his token number comes up and do the KYC,** accept the payment for opening in the form of cash/ on branch cheque and open the account by filling in only the mandatory six fields in the system. In case, the customer wants an non personalized welcome kit, the CR0 will hand over the non personalized welcome kit to the customer and direct him to the Grahak Mitra who will then demonstrate that the account is fully operational. In case the customer has opted for a personalized welcome kit, the CR0 will inform the customer that the personalized welcome kit will be delivered at his residence within 4 days and thank him for choosing to bank with SBH. The whole process of opening the account by the CR0 will not take more than 10 minutes.

c. **The form is then sent to LCPC (Liability CPC),** the inward dak desk will receive the form and send it to the scrutiny officer. After scrutinizing the form for completeness the officer will send the form to the scanning section where the signature of the account is scanned and uploaded in the system. The account opening form is then sent to the account opening section where the remaining data entry relating to the account is done. Account opening form is stored in the LCPC archival space for further usage.

d. **In case, the customer has opted for a personalized welcome kit,** a report will be downloaded by the welcome kit section in which the cheque book request for the customer is obtained. This is then sent to the printer who will print the cheque book for the customer and send to the welcome kit section. An ATM extract also goes to GE who prints the ATM cards and dispatches them to the welcome kit section. At the welcome kit section the welcome kit combining the ATM card, cheque book and welcome letter is compiled and dispatched to the customer address via speedpost.

e. **The welcome kit reaches the customer** within 4 days of filling out the form.

The benefits derived through this process are :

i. The opening of the account by the customer time comes down from –40 minutes earlier to 10 minutes.

ii. A fully functional account can be provided to the customer in 10 minutes if he chooses to opt for the non personalized welcome kit.

iii. The CR0 has to do only the minimum 6 six fields in the system and has more time to speak to the customer and cross sell other products to him.

2. **SARC (Stretched Assets Recovery Centre).** SARC Work can be categorized in the following roles :

f. **AGM (CRC) :**

i. Reviews all cases that are referred to CRC.

ii. Ensures full recovery of accounts.

iii. Approves proposals to be sent to ZCC for rehabilitation/recovery

g. **CM (Recovery) :**

i. Prepare/review proposals for hard recovery efforts.

ii. Ensure cases are filed within 30 days after transfer to Recovery cell.

iii. Monitor and guide case officers for recovery through civil suits and DRT. Also explore opportunities of compromise with borrowers.

h. **CM (Rehab/Recovery) :**

i. Prepares and reviews proposals made by city recovery officers.

ii. Provides expert opinion on exact course of action in rehabilitation/ restructuring efforts.

i. **CM Compromise :**

If request for compromise received, put it up to appropriate authority for consideration. He will not exercise any powers for compromise, as the accounts are handled by them.

For SARFAESI cases, guide case officer in the SARFAESI process. Arrange for physical possession of properties/ assets and arrange for auction of seized properties to recover the outstanding amount.

Explore opportunities of compromise with borrowers.

j. **City Case Officer :**

i. has end to end responsibility for all cases assigned to him.

ii. Liaison with lawyers/agents/advocates to ensure recovery.

iii. Monitor the account during the recovery period in the branches.

iv. Supported by award staff (fo1low up in courts) and enforcement agencies (pre litigation activities).

3. TFCPC (Trade Finance CPC) work can be divided into 3 main catogories:

k. Work handled at the branch/TFCPC front office : There are basically 3 units here :

1. **Inward Desk :**

i. Receives documents across the counter for LC/BG issuance, Export bills, and Inland bills.

ii. Manage multiple courier runs for load balancing in the back-office.

iii. Handle across the counter interactions on clarifications/discrepancies with customer personnel choosing to drop documents.

iv. Download the soft copies of email based LC/BG instructions by customers not using trade finance on the net.

v. Log new transactions in EXIM-Bills with date, time, stamp and place in queue with preference hierarchy.

vi. Handle non-credit customer application, indemnity and margin collection.

2. **Document Verification Unit**

i. Check incoming physical documents and soft copies for basic completeness and correctness.

ii. Note discrepancies on tracking system and on covering sheet for physical documents and hand-back to customer desk for check of physical delivery.

iii. Manage customer interaction on local phone for crucial discrepancies and clarifications.

iv. Clear and forward complaint documents/cases on system and physically to core operations in back-office

3. Customer Contact Unit

i. Manage inbound calls for customers on status of transactions and queries on alerts and internet messages.

ii. Manage outbound email updates and customer contacts for customers not using internet or alert facility.

2.26 Work handled at the TFCPC back office :

Back Office has various units under "Core Operations Section": LC Issuance, LC Advisory, Bank Guarantees, Import Bills, Export Bills and Forex and under "Service and Support Section": Swift, Returns, Record Maintenance, Accounting, Dispatch, IT Support, Facility Management, HR, Quality Assurance, Concurrent Audit. While the role of the service and support sections is rather self explanatory, core sections focus on delivering the following activities which form the backbone of TFCPC (depending on the Core Unit). It mainly looks into -

i. Ensure compliance with regulations RBI/FEMA/UCPDC/URC/EXIM .

ii. Ensure compliance with LC or P0 terms.

iii. Ensure compliance with credit sanction terms.

iv. Interact with RM team on charges/discrepancies/c1arifications/rate.

v. Interact with customer on charges/ discrepancies/clarifications/rates.

vi. Interact with advising bank on charges/discrepancies.

vii. Get rates from FX desk.

viii. Ensure compliance on requirements for R-returns.

ix. Ensure credit limit availability and compliance with terms of credit sanction for fund usage.

x. Ensure correct charges are levied.

xi. Ensure smooth information flow to foreign correspondent banks.

xii. Detailed scrutiny of import bil1s.

xiii. Interact with FD Calcutta on rates.

xiv. Booking and execution of forward contracts.

l. **Clearing CPC** : While most other BPR initiatives are geared towards improving customer experience, the Clearing CPC is one initiative that aims at providing relief to the branches. There is very little difference as far as the customers are concerned, but most of the clearing activity will move out of the branches. The procedure for Inward Clearing -

m. **Instruments will be received by the Clearing CPC** from the MICR center along with an RBI file containing instrument MICR line details.

n. **All the instruments will be scanned** and the images will be uploaded onto the system.

o. **For all instruments image based data** cleaning is done i.e. A/C numbers are entered for all instruments and Payee names are also entered for CC cheques.

p. **All the instruments are then posted** in CBS using the trickle feed mechanism.

q. **All the instruments for which the posting** failed in CBS for whatever reason (insufficient funds, Stop/Unstop instructions, instrument type and A/C type mismatch, cheque range not fed in CBS etc), will appear on the OLRR (Online Referral and Rejection) screens for branches I SMECC / AMG (A/C Management Group) who can then decide whether to honour/ reject the instrument. This must be done within cutoff time specified.

r. **Simultaneously, while the branches are clearing their OLRR** entries, the CCPC performs image based technical verification / passing of all instruments.

s. **At the cut-off time, all instruments that are rejected** either by the branches or during technical verification are separated, return memos prepared and the instruments are returned to the MICR- center.

Thus, the main benefit of the CCPC, apart from the time/cost saving and specialized work is that activity at the branches is reduced to just clearing the OLRR entries within cutoff time. Moreover, the process is more standardized resulting in consistency and greater accuracy. It also exploits technology more efficiently to improve efficiency in the clearing process.

2.27. Work Handled at Branch Office

Now turning to the other arm of clearing within the branches – i.e. outward clearing process, after a branch is linked to the Clearing CPC –

t. **Branches will open the drop-box** and count all the instruments and brand them with a crossing stamp, before handing them to a courier in a locked bag.

u. **The courier will carry the instruments** to the Clearing CPC, where the bags will be opened and the number of instruments cross checked with the number provided by the branch.

v. **The 'Clearing CPC will do** all the data entry (A/C number, amount, payee details etc) for all the outward clearing instruments received from the branches.

w. **All the instruments are then encoded** using power encoders and sent across to the MICR center.

The amount of outward clearing activity required to be done by the branches is now reduced to only counting of instruments from the drop-box, applying crossing-stamp and handing them to the courier in a locked bag.

2.28 Organizational Structure after Implementation of BPR at SBH

Implementation of BPR has also resulted in organization change process at State bank of Hyderabad:

Some of the major organizational changes that were initiated during the year 2004 :

New Position of Deputy Managing Director & Chief Economic Advisor : With economic reforms in the country gathering pace, the health of the economy and that of the financial system have become much more closely intertwined. In this environment, to enable the Bank to be in a position to anticipate various risks and evolve effective and pro-active mechanism towards risk management, the Bank created the position of chief Economic Adviser in the incumbency of Deputy Managing Director and the first incumbent joined the Bank in October 2004.

Creation of Mid Corporate Group : Mid corporate business was hived out of National Banking Group and consolidated in a new specialized Mid Corporate Group (MCG), created within the Corporate Banking Group SBU headed by Managing Director (CB). The MCG has already accelerated the growth of the Bank's Mid Corporate portfolio.

Stressed Assets Management Group : Stressed Assets Management Group has been created by the Bank within Corporate Banking Group to have an increased focus on speedy resolution of high value NPAs with dues of Rs. 5.00 crore and above.

Restructuring of NBG : New strategic business units were created for Personal Banking, Small & Medium Enterprises, Agriculture and Government business. Commercial and Retail Networks at the Circle level have been replaced by two Retail Networks. The new structure and Processes have helped achieve robust informal linkages and effective relationships between the Modules / Branches and the Business Unit. In another initiative, many Regional Offices which had been located at Module Head Quarters, have this year, been relocated to centres within their respective areas of operation as On Locale Regional Offices (OLROs). This has imparted better focus on business and customers.

The organizational set-up is represented by the Managing Director at the top assisted by the Chief General Manager and 6 General Managers are looking after the functions of operations, Commercial and International Banking, Planning & Development, Treasury, Inspection & vigilance; and Information & Technology. The Bank has 6 decentralized units i.e., Zonal Offices at Hyderabad, Secunderabad, Warangal, Vizag, Gulbarga and Aurangabad - and two independent Regional Offices at New Delhi and 51 Mumbai headed by Deputy General Managers. The Bank also has a Commercial Module comprising of branches dealing with high-value corporate business.

Transformed financial architecture — at the national and global levels — has significant implications for corporate strategy, organisation and performance, necessitating a move for banks to become 'one-stop financial shops'. This is what the commercial banks are aiming through their process re-engineering.

❖ ❖ ❖

CHAPTER - III

Impact of BPR on Performance of SBH

Banking all over the world during last decade witnessed changes which perhaps it did not see during its entire history. The changes are not only confined to developed countries. Banking in developing countries like ours has also started witnessing these changes. The changed technological and socio-economical factors, the emergence of new financial services has been provided with support of Information Technology, e.g. easy transfer of funds and messages across and beyond the national boundaries. Financial institutions, including banks, all over the world are, therefore, crucially dependent on products of IT and thus the need for BPR in banks.

Though the pace of change has been slow, yet the Indian banking scene is no exception to this phenomenon of transformation in products and services affected through IT. During the same period i.e. the last decade, with the liberalization and opening up of Indian Economy, new private sector banks were established. Foreign banks also expanded their presence in India. The new private sector banks had a distinct advantage over the nationalized banks as they were able to start their operations with fully computerized services from day one. Foreign Banks were already offering such services.

The Nationalized Banks, with their social obligations, were having a large number of branches operating manually and a huge customer base. But then the presence of new private and foreign banks with their attractive products and service packages, the customers had several options. The products offered by these banks lured the customers away from the banks which did not offer them. This set a new trend in banking industry. Retaining the existing customer base and expanding the same became the order of the day. The competition among the banks became very intense.

The leading banks, therefore, quickly shifted their focus by re-engineering their processes to providing prompt, efficient customer service and offering variety of hi-tech banking products/services. In order to achieve the same, the leading nationalized banks started building up necessary infrastructure for introducing attractive hi-tech products and offering new services. The profitability is related with productivity. There is direct relationship between productivity and profitability. An increase in productivity will increase the profitability and vice-versa.

Productivity may be defined as the output per unit of a factor of production in a given period. Productivity index thus tells us about the relationship between inputs and outputs in an enterprise. Productivity is a ratio of input and output. Productivity, in banking sector means the employee's efficiency, which has definite bearing on the profitability. As banking operations are influenced by govt. policy, RBI directives and various other socio-economic compulsions, it is difficult to set fixed parameters for productivity in banks. The parameters keep changing with the change in banking policy and differ according to the oranizational structure. Productivity can reveal a great deal about the future course of improvement or deterioration.

The chapter makes an attempt to study the impact of BPR on growth , productivity and profitability of SBH from 2000 to 2009.The first phase of BPR was rolled out in the year 2004 in SBH, and so the year 2004 is taken as the base year and index is calculated prior BPR (i.e.2000 to 2003) and post BPR (i.e.2005 to 2009).Though we are aware of the impact on growth, profits and productivity of a bank is depending on many factors, efforts are made to study the same keeping in view the growth rate of GDP in Indian economy for the above period and the analysis is been done and conclusions made .

Table 3.1

Growth rate in Indian Economy

Year	GDP	%
2000	5.45	100
2001	3.89	71
2002	4.56	84
2003	6.86	125
2004	7.89	145
2005	9.13	168
2006	9.75	179
2007	9.21	169
2008	7.9	145
2009	5.3	97

Source : International Monetary Fund - 2008 World Economic Outlook & Indian Express, Feb 27 2009

3.1 The Impact of BPR on the growth of SBH

The Impact of BPR on the growth of SBH is studied with respect to the no. of offices, no. of employees, deposits and advances of SBH from 2000 to 2009. The data is tabulated, analyzed and presented in tables 3.2 to 3.5.

3.1A No. of Offices : The table below indicates a gradual increase in the no. of offices from 2000 to 2009.

Table No 3.2

No. of offices

Year	No. of offices	Index
2000	1024	97
2001	1033	98
2002	1035	98
2003	1048	99.6
2004	1052	100
2005	1059	100.6
2006	1054	100.1
2007	1071	102
2008	1096	104
2009	1112	105.7

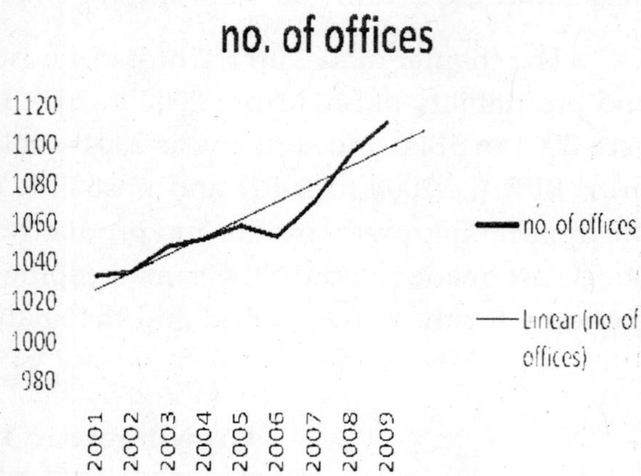

Source : State Bank of Hyderabad Annual Reports 1999-2000 to 2008-2009

During the pre Business Process Re-engineering (BPR) period (2000-2003) there was a gradual increase in Number of Offices i.e. from 1024 to 1052 offices being 2% growth rate whereas immediately a year of implementation of BPR we find a gradual decrease of 0.5% i.e. reduced to 1054 offices from that of 1059 offices. In the subsequent year of the post BPR period (i.e. 2005-2006), the year 2006-2007 saw an increase of 1.6% in the growth that the total number of offices being 1071.In 2008-2009 there is an increase of 5.7% with the total no of offices being 1112.

3.1B Number of employees : The table below indicates a decrease in the number of employees at SBH from 2000 to 2009.

Table 3.3

Number of Employees

Year	Number of Employees	Index
2000	14740	111
2001	13280	100
2002	13350	101
2003	13476	101
2004	13278	100
2005	13107	99
2006	13108	99
2007	12880	97
2008	12813	96
2009	12577	94.72

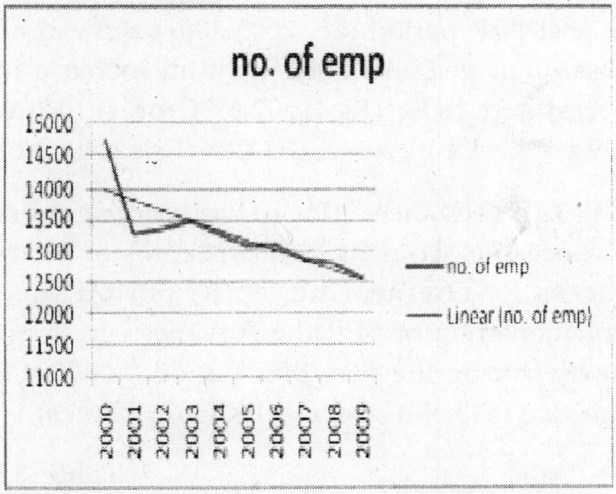

Source : State Bank of Hyderabad Annual Reports 1999-2000 to 2008-2009

The total Number of Employees were reducing gradually during the pre Business Process Re-engineering (BPR) period (2000-2003) i.e. from 14740 to 13476 showing an decrease by 11% in the growth rate whereas in the subsequent years of the post BPR period (i.e. 2004-2009) showed a decrease of only 5% i.e. from 13278 to 12577employees.

3.1C Deposits : The table below indicates the trends in the amount of deposits at SBH from 2000 to 2009

Table 3.4

Deposits (Rs/ In Crores)

Year	Deposits (Rs.in Chores)	Index
2000	12527	3
2001	14842	16
2002	17403	69
2003	20599	84
2004	25311	100
2005	28930	117
2006	34025	229
2007	41503	134
2008	50108	198
2009	62449	247

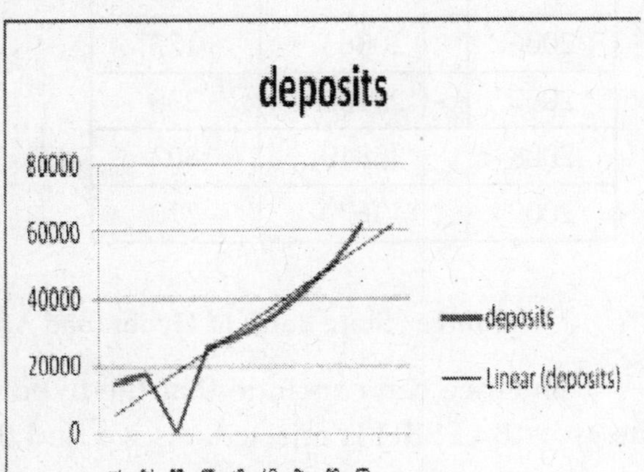

Source : State Bank of Hyderabad Annual Reports 1999-2000 to 2008-2009

During the pre Business Process Re-engineering (BPR) period (i.e. 2000-2003) The deposits were Rs.12527 crores (2000), decrease by 97%, Rs. 14842 Crores (2001) decrease by 84% compared to Rs.25311 Crores in the year 2004 (Implementation Year), whereas the post BPR period (i.e. 2005-2007) showed an increase 17% (Rs.28930 Crores) in the subsequent year i.e. 2005 with an increase in the growth rate by 129%(Rs.34024.6 Crores) and 180% (Rs.41502.67 Crores) in the year 2006 and 2007.In the year 2008-2009 we find a increase of 147% (Rs.62449 Crores) as compared to the base year 2004.

3.1D Advances : There has been a gradual increase by 20% in the growth rate of Advances i.e. from Rs. 6080.91Crores to Rs. 8422.58 Crores during the pre Business Process Re-engineering (BPR) period (i.e. 2000-2003) whereas in the year of implementation of BPR the Advances grew up by 29% i.e. (Rs.11813.68) with a rapid growth during the post BPR period (i.e. 2004-2009) showing an increase of 270% (i.e. from Rs.11813.68 Crores to Rs.43679 Crores) is shown in the table below.

Table 3.5

Advances (Rs. In Crores)

Year	Advances	Index
2000	6081	51
2001	7091	60
2002	8423	71
2003	9663	82
2004	11813	100
2005	15600	132
2006	20863	177
2007	28109	238
2008	35849	303
2009	43679	370

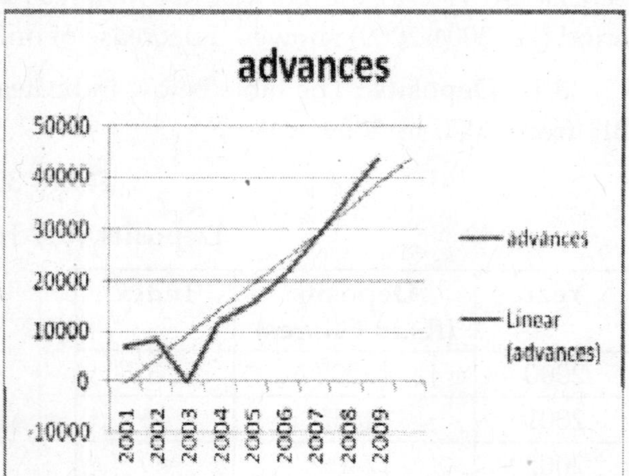

Source : State Bank of Hyderabad Annual Reports 1999-2000 to 2008-2009

Thus we can conclude that the hypothesis 1 - that there is no impact of BPR on the growth of SBH is rejected. As we find the following results :

1. In 2008-2009 there is an increase of 5.7% with the total no of offices being 1112 as compared to1052 offices in the base year 2004.

2. In the subsequent years of the post BPR period (i.e. 2004-2009) showed a decrease of 5%in the no. of employees i.e. from 13278 to 12577 employees. This can be attributed to increased efficiency of employees due to BPR at SBH.

3. In the year 2008-2009 we find a drastic increase of 147% of deposits (from Rs.25311crores in the year 2004 to Rs.62449 Crores) in 2009.

4. There is a rapid growth during the post BPR period (i.e. 2004-2009) showing an increase of 270% with respect to advances of the bank (i.e. from Rs.11813.68 Crores to Rs.43679 Crores).

All these factors can be attributed to the growth of SBH due to BPR.

3.2 The Impact of BPR on Productivity of SBH :

The impact of productivity of SBH is studied with the help of productivity per employee, productivity per branch and NPA ratios.

Productivity per employee is ascertained by: 1) Business per employee, 2) Profits per employee 3) Deposits per employee and 4) Advances per employee.

Productivity per branch is evaluated by: 5) Business per branch, 6) Deposits per branchand7) Advances per branch.

The quality of loans/Advances of the bank is assessed by: 8) Gross NPA's as percentage to advances, 9) Gross NPA's as percentage to total assets, 10) Net NPA's as percentage to advances and 11) Net NPA's as percentage to total assets are computed and analyzed and presented in the following pages.

3.2A Productivity Per employee

The impact of BPR on productivity of SBH is analyzed with the help of data relating to Business per employee, profit per employee, advances per employee and deposits per employee as it measures the efficiency in use of human capital. These ratios are computed for the years 2000 to 2009 and presented in tables 3.6 to 3.9.

Table 3.6

Business per Employee

Year	Business per Employee (Rs in Lakhs)	Index
2000	126.24	47
2001	165.16	62
2002	166.04	62
2003	226.20	85
2004	265.86	100
2005	339.74	128
2006	418.73	158
2007	540.47	203
2008	599.08	225
2009	839.82	316

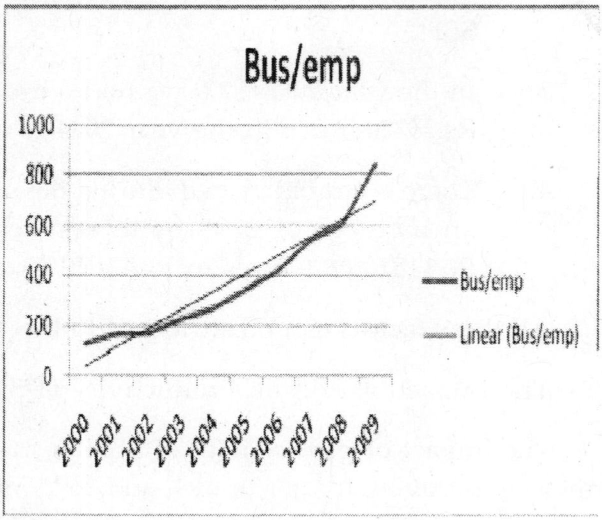

Source : State Bank of Hyderabad Annual Reports 1999-2000 to 2008-2009

The trend of 'Business per Employee' shows gradual increase during the pre Business Process Re-engineering -BPR period (2000-2003) with a growth rate of 44% (i.e. from Rs.126.24 Lakhs to Rs.227.23 Lakhs). The business was Rs.279.59 Lakhs in the year 2004 (the year of implementation of BPR). Thereafter, it increased to Rs.839.82 Crores during the post BPR period (2004-2009) with a rapid increase of 216%.

Table - 3.7

Profit per Employee

Year	Profit per employee (Rs. in Crores)	Index
2000	0.87	30
2001	1.13	39
2002	1.68	59
2003	2.25	78
2004	2.87	100
2005	1.91	67
2006	3.26	114
2007	3.92	137
2008	4.35	152
2009	4.87	170

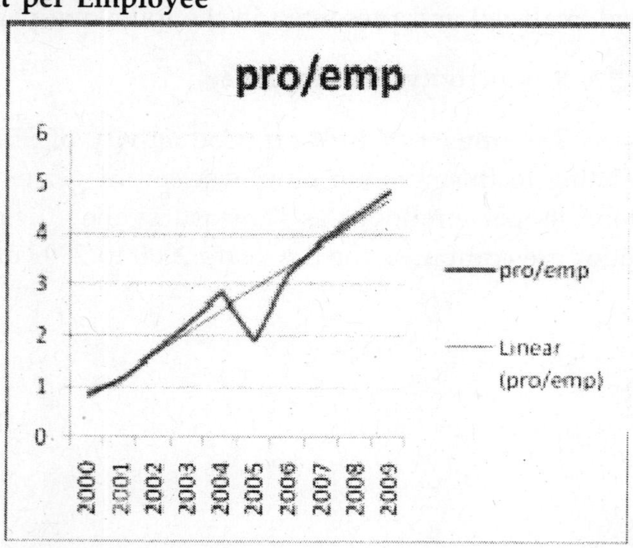

Source : State Bank of Hyderabad Annual Reports 1999-2000 to 2008-2009

The trend of 'Profit per Employee' shows gradual increase during the pre Business Process Re-engineering -BPR period (200)-2003) with a growth rate of 70% (i.e. from Rs.0.87 Crores to Rs.2.87 Crores). The Profits were Rs.2.87 Crores in the year 2004 (the year of implementation of BPR). Thereafter, it increased to Rs.4.87 Crores during the post BPR period (2004-2009) with a rapid increase of 170%.

Table 3.8

Advances per Employee

Year	Advances per Employee (Rs. in Crores)	Index
2000	0.41	46.07
2001	0.53	59.55
2002	0.63	71.59
2003	0.72	81.82
2004	0.89	100
2005	1.19	135.23
2006	1.59	180.6
2007	2.18	247.7
2008	2.79	315.9
2009	3.47	394.33

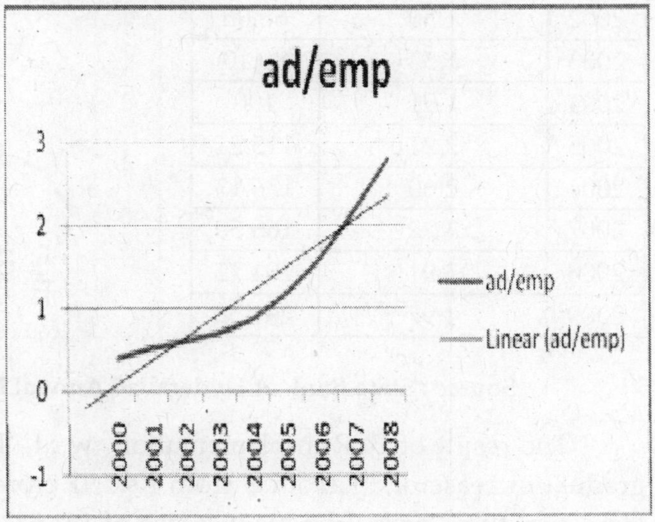

Source : State Bank of Hyderabad Annual Reports 1999-2000 to 2008-2009

The trend of 'Advances per Employee' shows gradual increase during the pre Business Process Re-engineering -BPR period (2000-2003) with a growth rate of 35% (i.e. from Rs.0.41 Crores to Rs.0.72 Crores). The Advances was Rs.0.89 Crores in the year 2004 (the year of implementation of BPR). Thereafter, it increased to Rs. 3.47 Crores during the post BPR period (2004-2009) with a rapid increase of 294.33%.

Table 3.9

Deposits per Employee

Year	Deposits per Employee (Rs. in Crores)	Index
2000	0.85	44.5
2001	1.11	58.12
2002	1.30	68.06
2003	1.53	80.10
2004	1.91	100
2005	2.21	115.21
2006	2.60	136.13
2007	3.22	168.59
2008	3.91	204.71
2009	4.97	261.58

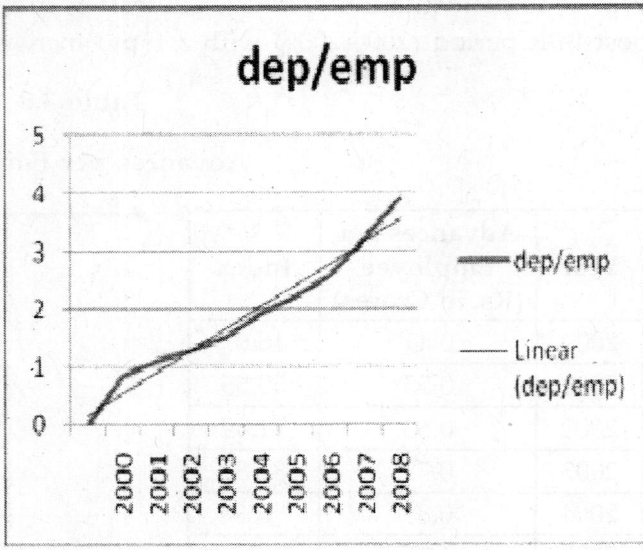

Source : State Bank of Hyderabad Annual Reports 1999-2000 to 2008-2009

The result of BPR implementation w.r.t. 'Deposits per Employee' has shown a gradual increase of 15.21% i.e. from Rs.1.91 crores to Rs. 2.21 crores in the year 2005. However, there was a drastic increase of 161.58% (i.e. from Rs. 1.91 crores to Rs. 4.97 crores) during post BPR period (2005-2009).

3.2B Productivity per branch

To measure branch productivity, three main ratios:1) total advances / loans per branch ,2) total deposits per branch and business per branch from2000 to 2009 are analyzed. These ratios reflect the effectiveness of bank branches in carrying out their primary functions in lending and mobilizing deposits. The ratios are computed and presented in tables 3.10

Table - 3.10

Business per Branch

Year	Business (Rs. in Crores)	Index
2000	21.49	53
2001	25.17	62
2002	29.27	73
2003	34.0	84
2004	40.35	100
2005	48.3	120
2006	59.07	146
2007	73.09	181
2008	87.72	217
2009	105.06	260

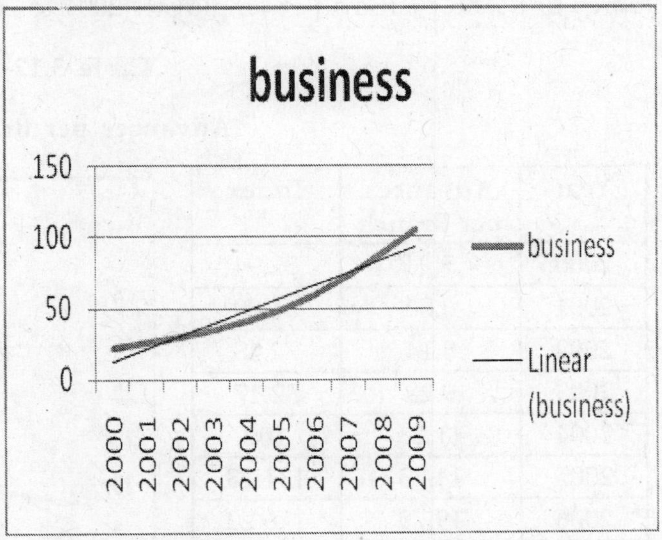

Source : State Bank of Hyderabad Annual Reports 1999-2000 to 2008-2009

The above data shows that the 'Business per Branch' had a gradual increase i.e. 31% of growth rate during the pre BPR period (i.e. from Rs. 21.49 crores to Rs. 34 crores). During the post BPR period, the business had a rapid increase of 81% (i.e. from Rs. 40.35 crores to Rs. 105.06 crores).

Table 3.11

Deposits per Branch

Year	Deposits per Branch	Index
2000	12.23	50.96
2001	14.37	59.75
2002	16.81	69.90
2003	19.66	81.75
2004	24.06	100
2005	27.32	113.56
2006	32.28	134.22
2007	38.75	161.12
2008	45.72	190.10
2009	56.16	233.51

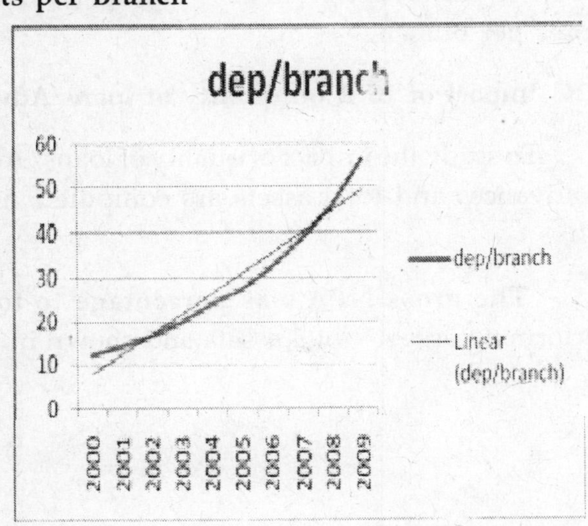

Source : State Bank of Hyderabad Annual Reports 1999-2000 to 2008-2009

We find almost 50% increase in deposits per branch during pre BPR period.Where as there is 133.51% of increase in deposits per branch after BPR i.e. fromRs. 24.06 crores to Rs. 56.16crores per employee (2004 to 2009)during post BPR period.

Table 3.12

Advances per Branch

Year	Advances per Branch	Index
2000	5.94	52.94
2001	6.86	61.09
2002	8.14	72.48
2003	9.22	82.17
2004	11.23	100
2005	14.73	131.28
2006	19.79	176.22
2007	26.25	233.75
2008	32.70	291.27
2009	39.28	349.78

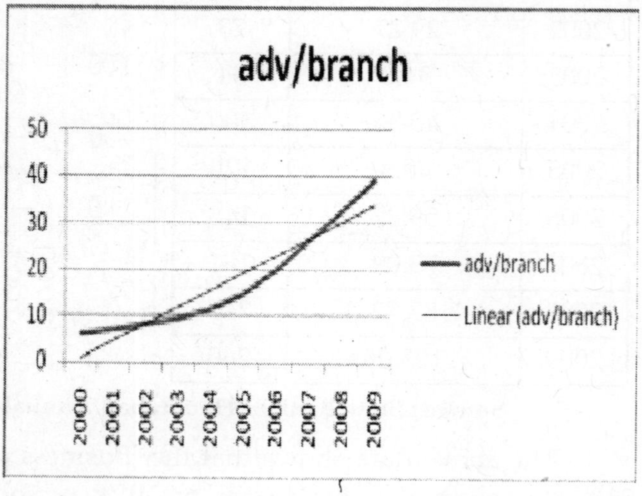

Source : State Bank of Hyderabad Annual Reports 1999-2000 to 2008-2009

The advances per branch shows a greater increase as compared to deposits per branch after the implementation of BPR in the year 2004.We find an increase of 250%in advances per branch from 2004 to 2009 i.e. from Rs.11.23 crores per branch to Rs.39.28 crores per branch.

3.2C Impact of BPR on quality of loans/Advance

To study the impact of quality of loans/Advances of the bank, NPA's as percentage to advances and total assets are computed, analyzed and presented in tables 3.13 to 3.16.

The gross NPA's as percentage to total assets are computed - Gross non-performing assets/ total assets and shown in table 3.13

Table 3.13

Gross Non Performing Assets (NPA'S) as Percentage to Total Assets

Year	Gross NPA (%)	Index
2000	6.03	267
2001	5.84	258
2002	4.06	180
2003	2.83	125
2004	2.26	100
2005	1.58	70
2006	1.12	50
2007	0.72	32
2008	0.51	23

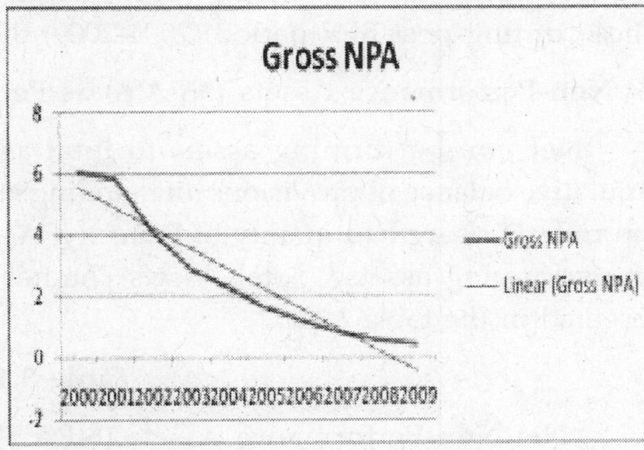

Source : Appendix Table III.28 Report on Trend & Progress of Banking in India, RBI Bulletin

There has been a almost a 4.20% decline in the growth rate of the Gross NPA as a percentage to Total Assets i.e. it has decreased from 6.03% to 2.83% during the pre Business Process Re-engineering (BPR) period (2000-2003) whereas the change that is noticed during post BPR period (2004-2009) there is a decrease of 77%.

The gross NPA's as percentage to advances are computed - Gross non-performing assets/ advances and shown in table 3.14

Table 3.14

Gross Non Performing Assets (NPA's) as Percentage to Advances

Year	Gross NPA (%)	Index
2000	14.18	253
2001	14.08	251
2002	10.08	180
2003	7.28	130
2004	5.6	100
2005	3.46	62
2006	2.14	38
2007	1.24	22
2008	0.87	16

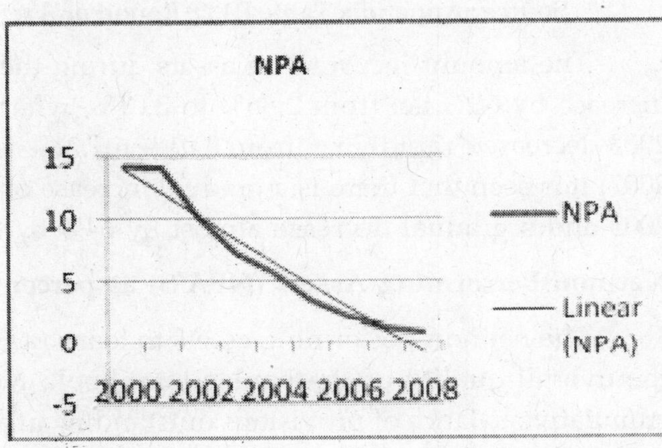

Source : Appendix Table III.28 Report on Trend & Progress of Banking in India, RBI Bulletin

There has been a almost a 4.20% decline in the growth rate of the Gross NPA as a percentage to Total Assets i.e. it has decreased from 6.03% to 2.83% during the pre Business Process Re-engineering (BPR) period (2000-2003) whereas the change that is noticed during post BPR period (2004-2009) there is a decrease of 84%.

Net Non-Performance Assets (NPA'S) as Percentage to total Assets

Net non-performing assets to total assets ratio are calculated by reducing cumulative balance of provisions outstanding at a period end from gross NPAs. Higher, ratio reflects rising bad quality of loans. NPA as percentage to total assets ratio = Net non-performing assets/ Total Assets.The net NPA to total assets is computed and presented in the table 3.15

Table 3.15

Net Non-Performance Assets (NPA'S) as Percentage to total Assets

Year	Net NPA (%)	Index
2000	2.86	1144
2001	3.01	1204
2002	1.89	756
2003	1.21	484
2004	0.25	100
2005	0.27	108
2006	0.19	76
2007	0.12	48
2008	0.09	36

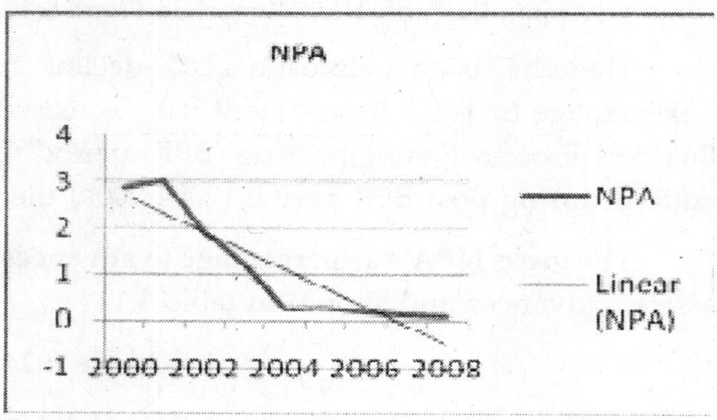

Source : Appendix Table III.28 Report on Trend & Progress of Banking in India

The amount incurred on assets during the pre BPR period of 2000-2001 had an increase by 60% i.e. from 2.86% to 3.01%, whereas, the NPA during the years 2001-2003 decreased rapidly i.e. from 3.01% to1.21% and during the post BPR period (2004-2007) it is seen that there is a gradual increase of 8% in the subsequent year of BPR i.e. 2005 and a gradual decrease almost by 64% by 2008.

Net non Performing Assets (NPA'S) as percentage to Advances

The net non-performing assets to loans (advances) ratio are used as a measure of the overall quality of the bank's loan book. Net NPAs are calculated by reducing cumulative balance of provisions outstanding at a period end from gross NPAs. Higher ratio reflects rising bad quality of loans. NPA ratio = Net non-performing assets/ Advances

Table 3.16

Net non Performing Assets (NPA'S) as percentage to Advances

Year	Net NPA (%)	Index
2000	7.3	1123
2001	7.83	1205
2002	4.96	763
2003	3.26	502
2004	0.65	100
2005	0.61	94
2006	0.36	55
2007	0.22	34
2008	0.16	25
2009	0.38	58

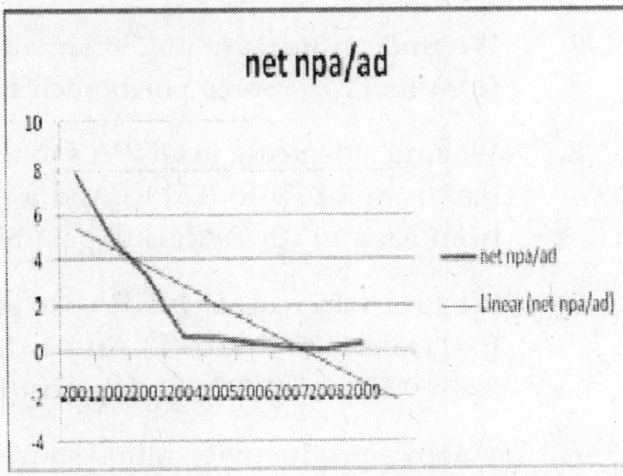

Source : Appendix Table III.28 Report on Trend & Progress of Banking in India

It has been observed from the above table that the net NPA have increased from 7.30% to 7.83% (i.e. 0.50%) during 2000-2001, there has been a decline by around 4.57% during the year 2001-2003 that is from 7.83 to 3.26 during the pre Business Process Re-engineering (BPR) period, when compared to a decrease of 66 % (i.e. from 0.65 to 0.22), during post BPR period (2004-2007). There is a net decrease of NPA by 42% in the year 2009 as compared to the base year 2004.

Thus we can conclude that-

H2 –there is no impact of BPR on productivity of SBH is also tested and rejected because,

1. The business per employee was Rs.265.86 Lakhs in the year 2004 (the year of implementation of BPR). Thereafter, it increased to Rs.839.82 lakhs during the post BPR period (2004-2009) we find a rapid increase of 216%.

2. There is 70% of increase with respect to profit per employee i.e from Rs.2.87 crores to Rs.4.87 crores per employee during post BPR period (2004 to 2009).

3. The Advances per employee was Rs.0.89 Crores in the year 2004, thereafter, it increased to Rs.3.47 Crores during 2009 with an increase of 294.33%.

4. The deposits per employee there was a drastic increase of 161.58% (i.e. from Rs.1.91 crores to Rs.4.97 crores) during post BPR period (2005-2009).

5. Business per branch during the post BPR period, the business showed an increase of 160% (i.e. from Rs. 40.35 crores to Rs. 105.06 crores).

6. There is 133.51% of increase in deposits per branch after BPR i.e. from Rs. 24.06 crores to Rs. 56.16crores per employee (2004 to 2009).

7. We find an increase of 250%in advances per branch from 2004 to 2009i.e. from Rs.11.23 crores per branch to Rs.39.28 crores per branch.

8. We find a decrease in GNPA's to total assets by 77%during post BPR period (i.e. from 2.26% to 0.51%).And a decrease of 84% in GNPA's to advances from 5.6% to 0.87% during post BPR period.

9. We find a decrease in NNPA's to total assets by 64%during post BPR period (i.e. from 0.25 to 0.09%).And a decrease of 42% in NNPA's to advances from 0.65% to 0.38% during post BPR period

All the above productivity ratios shows a very impressive performance of the bank as we find the dramatic change of more than 125% during post BPR period reflecting on the impact of BPR on productivity of the branch.

3.3 Impact of BPR on Profitability Ratios :

To assess the profitability of SBH during pre and post BPR period the following ratios are calculated, analyzed and presented. 1)Capital adequacy ratio, 2)Operating Expenses as a Percentage to Total Assets,3) Interest income as percentage of total assets,4) Interest expended as percentage of total assets, 5)Net interest income as percentage of total assets,6) Gross profit / loss as percentage of total assets and7) Net profit / loss as percentage of total assets

3.3A Capital adequacy ratio (CAR) :

CAR is calculated as a bank's capital ratio is the ratio of qualifying capital to risk adjusted (or weighted) assets. The RBI has set the minimum capital adequacy ratio at 10% for all banks. A ratio below the minimum indicates that the bank is not adequately capitalized to expand its operations. The ratio ensures that the bank do not expand their business without having adequate capital. This is in accordance with the Basel II norms, CAR = (Tier I capital + Tier II capital)/ Risk weighted assets

Table 3.17

Capital Adequacy Ratio (CAR)

Year	CAR (%)	Index
2000	10.86	76
2001	12.28	86
2002	14.03	98
2003	14.91	104
2004	14.29	100
2005	11.74	82
2006	12.08	85
2007	12.51	88
2008	12.35	86
2009	10.58	74.05

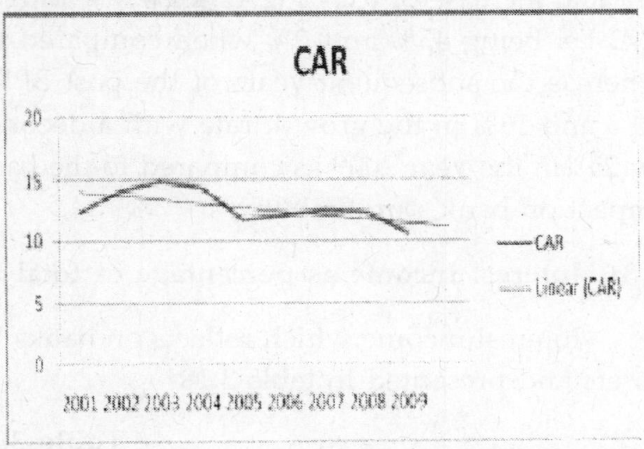

Source : **Appendix Table III.28 Report on Trend & Progress of Banking in India**

The pre Business Process Re-engineering (BPR) period (2000-2003) showed a gradual increase i.e. from 10.86 to 14.91 being 28% in the growth rate of Capital Adequacy Ratio (CAR) whereas the subsequent year of the post BPR period (i.e. 2004-2005) showed a decrease of 28% with an increase in the growth rate by 5% during the year 2005-2007.In the current year the CAR has decreased by 11% as compared to the previous year because the bank had to adopt Basel II norms.

3.3B Operating Expenses as a Percentage to Total Assets

This ratio explains the operational efficiency of the bank. The operating expenses are placed in relation to its total assets. The operating expenses as percentage to total assets are computed for the years 2000 to 2009 and presented in the table 3.18

Table 3.18

Operating Expenses as a Percentage to Total Assets

Year	Operating Expenses	Index
2000	2.42	139
2001	2.46	141
2002	1.88	108
2003	1.73	99
2004	1.74	100
2005	1.92	110
2006	2.01	116
2007	1.65	95
2008	1.30	75

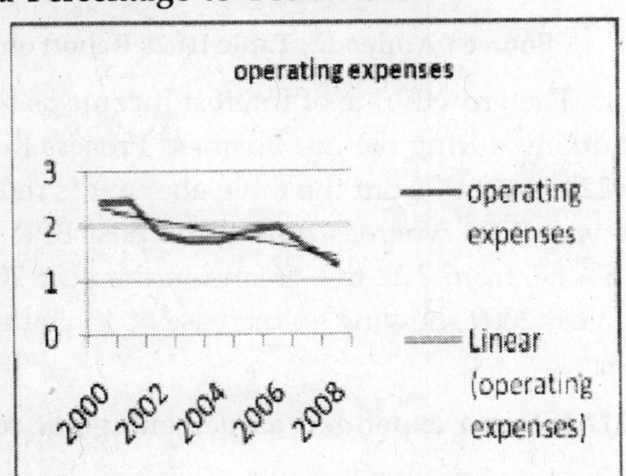

Source : **Appendix Table III.28 Report on Trend & Progress of Banking in India**

There is a lot of fluctuation in the operating expenses, it can be seen that during the pre Business Process Re-engineering (BPR) period (i.e. 2000-2001) there has been a gradual increase of 0.03% (2.42 to2.45) with a decline in 2002 and 2003 being 1.88 and 1.73 i.e. being 43% and 2% when compared to the implantation year (2004's 1.74%) whereas the subsequent years of the post BPR period (2005-2006) saw an increase by 10% and 16% in the growth rate with a decline by 5% by 2007.And it further reduced by 25%in the year 2009 as compared to the base year 2004 thus indicating the positive impact on bank's profitability.

3.3C Interest income as percentage of total assets :

Interest income which reflects on banks business is compared in relation to total assets and presented in table 3.19

Table 3.19

Interest income as percentage of total assets

Year	Interest Income (%)	Index
2000	9.56	132
2001	9.19	127
2002	8.67	120
2003	7.91	110
2004	7.22	100
2005	6.66	92
2006	6.77	94
2007	6.85	95
2008	7.15	99

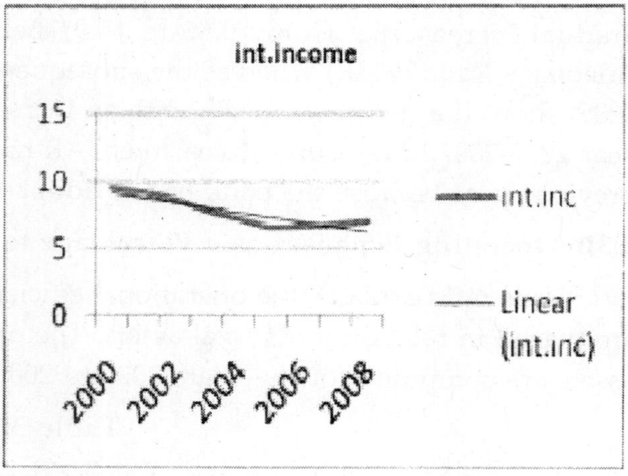

Source : Appendix Table III.28 Report on Trend & Progress of Banking in India

The growth rate of Interest Income as Percentage of Total Assets is seen declining gradually during the pre Business Process Re-engineering (BPR) period (2000-2003) i.e. by 22% as seen from the table above it is reduced from 9.56 in the year 2000 to 7.91 in the year 2003 whereas during the post BPR period (i.e. 2004-2005) showed a decrease of 6% i.e. from 7.22 to 6.66 and in the year 2006 it has increased to 6.77% and 7.15% in the year 2009 showing an increase of 4% in the growth rate as compared to the previous year.,

3.3D Interest expended as percentage of total assets :

Expenditure incurred on interest is compared to total assets and presented in table 3.20

Table 3.20

Interest expended as percentage of total assets

Year	Interest expended (%)	Index
2000	6.21	139
2001	5.88	131
2002	5.74	128
2003	5.05	113
2004	4.48	100
2005	3.9	87
2006	4.07	91
2007	4.35	97
2008	5.34	119

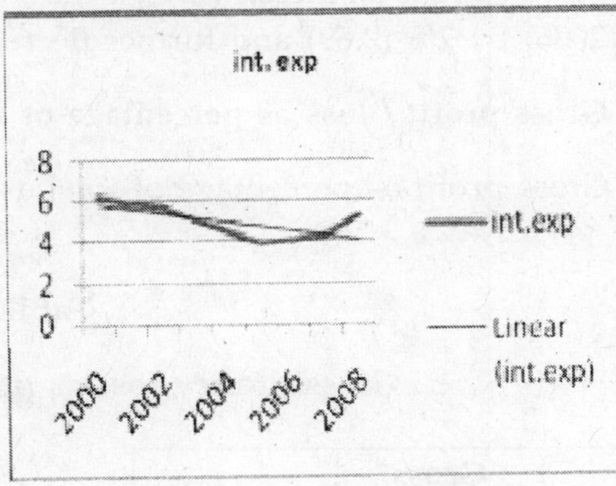

Source: Appendix Table III.28 Report on Trend & Progress of Banking in India

There is a decrease of 26% in the growth rate of Interest Expended as Percentage of Total Assets pre Business Process Re-engineering (BPR) period (2000-2003) se i.e. it is reduced from 6.21% to 5.05% whereas in the subsequent year of the implementation of BPR period there has been 13% i.e. from 4.48% to 3.9% during 2004-2005 and increase by 4% i.e. in 2006 and 6% in 2007 with an increase in the growth rate by 19% during post period of BPR (2004-2009).

3.3E Net interest income as percentage of total assets :

The difference between interest income and interest expense is compared to total assets and presented in table 3.21

Table 3.21

Net interest income as percentage of total assets

Year	Net interest income (%)	Index
2000	3.35	122
2001	3.32	121
2002	2.94	107
2003	2.86	104
2004	2.75	100
2005	2.76	101
2006	2.69	98
2007	2.50	91
2008	1.81	66

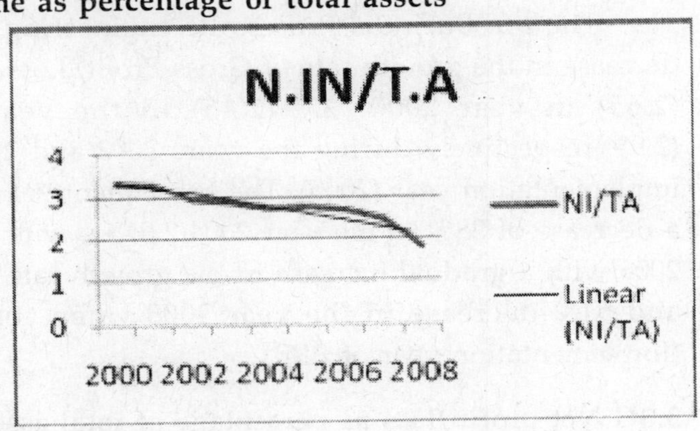

Source: Appendix Table III.28 Report on Trend & Progress of Banking in India

The pre Business Process Re-engineering (BPR) period (2000-2003) showed a gradual increase 18% (i.e. from 3.35 to 2.86) in the growth rate of Net Interest Income/ Margin as Percentage of Total Assets whereas in the immediate year (2005) of the post BPR period there is an increase by 1% (2.75 to 2.76) and then decrease in the subsequent year (2006) by 2% (2.69) and further decreased 33%(1.81) in the year 2009.

3.3F Gross profit / loss as percentage of total assets :

Gross profit as percentage of total assets is computed and analyzed from table 3.22

Table 3.22

Gross profit / loss as percentage of total assets

Year	Gross profit/ loss (%)	Index
2000	2.65	80
2001	2.43	73
2002	2.71	82
2003	2.9	88
2004	3.31	100
2005	2.04	62
2006	1.81	65
2007	2.05	62
2008	1.61	49

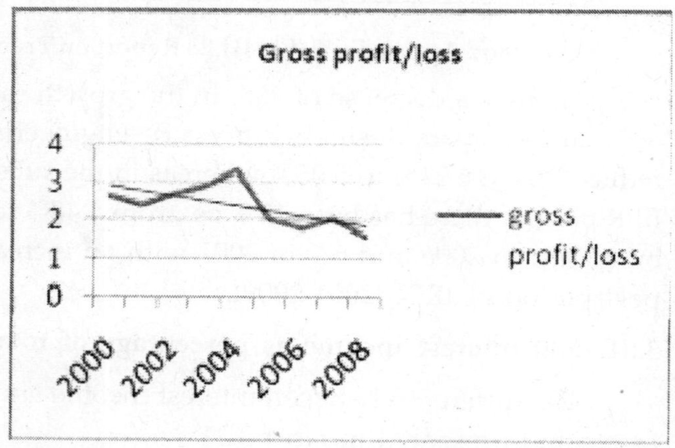

Source: Appendix Table III.28 Report on Trend & Progress of Banking in India

The pre Business Process Re-engineering (BPR) period (2000-2003) showed a decrease in the growth rate of Gross Profit/Loss as Percentage of Total Assets by 20% (2.65) in year 2000, 27%(2.43) in the year 2001 with 18%(2.71) and 12% (2.9%)respectively during the years 2002 and 2003 when compared to 3.31% in the implementation year (2005). The subsequent year of the post BPR period also showed a decrease of 38% in the year 2004(2.04%), with a further decrease to 45% (1.81%) in 2006 with a gradual increase in the growth rate by 0.76% compared to the year 2006 and 51% decrease in the year 2008 when compared to 3.31% in the year 2004 (Implementation year of BPR).

3.3G Net profit /loss as percentage of total assets :

Net profit as percentage of total assets is computed and analyzed from table 3.22

Table 3.23

Net profit / loss as percentage of total assets

Year	Net profit / loss (%)	Index
2000	0.82	66
2001	0.82	66
2002	1.02	82
2003	1.15	93
2004	1.24	100
2005	0.72	58
2006	1.05	85
2007	1.03	83
2008	0.90	73

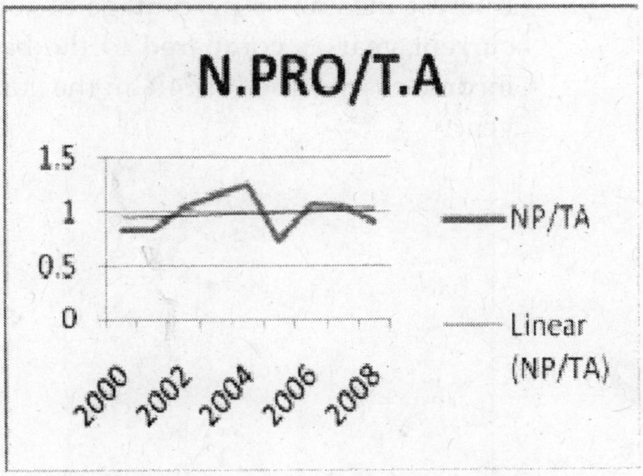

Source : Appendix Table III.28 Report on Trend & Progress of Banking in India

During the pre Business Process Re-engineering (BPR) period (2000-2003) the above table shows that there has been decrease in Net Profit/Loss as Percentage of Total Assets i.e. by 34%(0.82%), with 18%(1.02) and 3%(1.15) decrease during the years 2002 and 2003 when compared to 1.24% in the year 2004 the year of implementation of BPR. The growth rate during the post BPR period (i.e. 2004-2005) showed a decrease of 42% with an increase in the growth rate by 33% (1.05) in the year 2006 when compared to 0.72 in the year 2005 with a gradual decrease by 2% (1.03) in the year 2007and further declined by 10%in the year 2008 compared to 1.24 during the year 2004.

Thus we can conclude that-

H3 - There is no impact of BPR on profitability of SBH is accepted.

1. There is a gradual decrease in net profits to total assets during post BPR period as we find a decrease of 27% decrease i.e from Rs.1.24%of total assets in 2004 to 0.90% of total assets in 2009.

2. There is 51% decrease in gross profits to total assets during 2004 to 2009 i.e. from 3.31% of total assets to 1.61% of total assets.

3. Net interest income as percentage of total assets also reduced during post BPR period by 34% (from 2.45% to 1.81% net interest income to total assets)

4. Interest expended as percentage of total assets has increase by 19% during 2004 to 2009 i.e from 4.48% to 5.34% of interest spent as percentage to total assets. An increase in expenses shows a reduction in the profit margin.

5. Interest income as percentage of total assets has decreased by 1% in the current year as compared to the base year. It is also found that interest income as increased by 4% in the current year as compared to the previous year.

❖ ❖ ❖

CHAPTER - IV

Impact of BPR at SBH on Employees - Analysis of employees perceptions

In banking institution an employee constitute the most important input. Because of this fact, the concern for improving productivity has to be focused on staff productivity also.

In this chapter an attempt is made to examine the views and perceptions of bank employees. The responses of 125 bank employees of State Bank of Hyderabad was collected, analyzed and discussed in detail. After the pilot survey it was found that all the employees in the bank are not aware of BPR in at their bank and it was only branch manager and assistant manager were able to give information. Thereby the structured questionnaires were executed only to these two cadres in the bank to know the perceptions of the employees in relation to Business Process Reengineering in banks focusing on issues relating to -

1) Objectives of BPR in banks (employees perceptions of the same).
2) Awareness among the employees of BPR initiatives taken up by the bank.
3) Level of satisfaction of the employees with respect to BPR initiatives at SBH.
4) Impact of information technology on employees.
5) BPR's impact on customers, employees and bank as perceived by employees.
6) Employees perceptions with regard to banking services before and after BPR.
7) Benefits of BPR to the employees.
8) Problems faced by employees due to BPR.

For the convenience of discussion the chapter is divided into 2 sections. Section - A presents the profile of sample employees and section - B presents analysis of employees perceptions on BPR in SBH.

Part A

4.1 Profile of Sample Employees

The profile of 125 employees of SBH has been taken as a sample for the study and presented in the table below.

Table 4.01

Age wise distribution of sample respondents

S.No.	Profile	Variables	Frequency	%
1	Age	25 to 50 years	110	88
		>50 years	15	12
		Total	125	100

Source : Primary data

Age wise composition clearly states that the majority of the respondents (88%) of them are in the middle age group i.e. between 25 to 50 years and the rest of them are above 50 years.

Table 4.02

Gender vs Sample respondents

S.No.	Profile	Variables	Frequency	%
2	Gender	Male	79	63.2
		Female	46	36.8
		Total	125	100.0

Source : Primary data

63.2% of the respondents are male and the remaining 36.8% are female employees

Table 4.03

Educational Qualification of Sample Employees

S.No.	Profile	Variables	Frequency	%
3	Educational Qualification	SSC & below	1	.8
		Graduate	94	75.2
		Post Graduate	30	24.0
		Total	125	100.0

Source : Primary data

Three forth majority of the respondents (75.2%) are graduates, 24% of them are post graduates and only 1 respondent was an SSC qualified.

Table 4.04

Designation vs Sample Employee

S.No.	Profile	Variables	Frequency	%
4	Designation	Asst Manager	78	62.4
		Br. Manager	47	37.6
		Total	125	100.0

Source : Primary data

Designation wise sample employees include assistant managers (62.4%) and branch managers (37.6%).

Table 4.05

Computer Knowledge of Sample Respondents

S.No.	Profile	Variables	Frequency	%
5	Computer Knowledge	Software	79	63.2
		Hardware	4	3.2
		Both	5	4.0
		None	37	39.6
		Total	125	100.0

Source : Primary data

63.2% of the sample respondents were aware of software used in the bank, 39.6% of the respondents are computer illiterate, 3.2% of the respondents knew hard ware and only 4% of the respondents were aware of the both.

Table 4.06

Experience vs Sample Employees

S.No.	Profile	Variables	Frequency	%
6	Experience	Less than 5 yrs	35	28.0
		5 to 10 yrs	11	8.8
		Above 10 yrs	79	63.2
		Total	125	100.0

Source : Primary data

63.2% of the respondents were having more than 10 years of experience in the bank, 28% of them were working for less than 5 years and the remaining respondents were between 5 to10 years of experience.

Table 4.07

Annual Income wise Distribution of Sample Respondents

S.No.	Profile	Variables	Frequency	%
7	Annual Income	Less than 5 lakhs	122	97.6
		5.01--10.00 lakhs	3	2.4
		Total	125	100.0

Source : Primary data

Income wise analysis reveals that, (97.6%) of the respondents are in the income group of less than Rs. 5 lakhs per annum and the remaining 2.4% are earning aboveRs. 5 lakhs to Rs. 10 lakhs per annum

Part B

Employee Perceptions

The chapter analyses the perceptions of 125 employees of state bank of Hyderabad of various branches to study the impact of BPR on its employees. The sample employees are selected mainly from four major cities namely Hyderabad, Khammam, Warangal and Karimnagar. After the pilot survey it was found that all the employees in the bank are not aware of BPR in their banks and it was only branch manager and assistant manager were able to give information. Thereby 15 branches in each of these four cities were selected and the data was collected from both the assistant and branch managers along with 5 employees of BPR unit at SBH, thus the sample of employees constitute 125 in number (i.e.4×15×2+5).

The study includes analysis of employees perceptions, on objectives of BPR at SBH, awareness regarding the basic knowledge of BPR initiatives, benefits of BPR, level of satisfaction of employees with respect to BPR at their banks, its impact on customers, employees and on bank performance as perceived by employees, problems faced by the employees due to BPR in their bank if any.

4.2 Objective of BPR as perceived by the employees of SBH

The year 2004 was the designing phase for BPR at State Bank of Hyderabad with the following objectives.

1. Simplify customer facing branch processes.
2. Migrate non-customer facing processes to central processing centres.
3. Empower branches to become sales, service and marketing units.
4. Raise customer satisfaction levels
5. To enhance productivity

Efforts are being made to examine the perceptions of bank employees as it is important to know whether the employees are working towards these objectives, for the effective functioning of the bank. In order to know the perceptions of the employees, they were asked to rank the objectives according to their preference. Their responses have been analyzed and presented in table 4.2

Table 4.2

Objective of BPR in banks - Employees perceptions

S.No.	Particulars	Weighted Score	Average Score	Rank
1	Cost reduction in operations	866	6.93	5
2	Accuracy of transactions	887	7.10	4
3	Speedy operations	1069	8.55	1
4	Better customer services	1054	8.43	2
5	Adoption of latest technology	927	7.42	3
6	Reducing cost of employees	518	4.14	9
7	Reduction of staff	394	3.15	11
8	Easy rectification of errors	511	4.09	10
9	To satisfy existing customers	694	5.55	6
10	To create new customers	664	5.31	7
11	To win over competitors	572	4.58	8
	Total	8156	5.93	-

Source : Primary data

The employees considered speedy operations with a maximum average score of 8.55 as the major objective of BPR in banks. In the order of priority the other objectives include, better customer services (8.43), adoption of latest technology (7.42), accuracy of transactions (7.10) and cost reduction in operations (6.93).to satisfy existing customers

(5.55) and to create new customers (5.31) and the least importance is given to easy rectification of errors and reduction of staff.

4.3 Awareness among employees with respect to BPR in Banks

As it is important that the employees should be aware of the various BPR initiatives taken by the bank, and the changes that is required in their job description. An analysis is made with respect to the awareness of various changes among the sample respondents, the employees were asked to express their level of awareness of different aspects on three point scale with the responses, fully aware, partly aware and not aware. The responses are tabulated and presented below in table 4.3.

Table 4.3

Employees awareness on BPR initiatives at SBH

S.No.	Particulars	Not Aware	Partly aware	Fully Aware	Total
1	Back-end software used for banking operations	25	89	11	125
	% of respondents	20	71.2	8.8	100
2	Recommendations of Information technology in the banks	11	79	35	125
	% of respondents	8.8	63.2	28	100
3	Knowledge about electronic services offered by banks	4	77	44	125
	% of respondents	3.2	61.6	35.2	100
4	Hardware knowledge to correct simple technical snags	48	62	15	125
	% of respondents	38.4	49.6	12.0	100
5	Retail banking i.e. CPC's	18	63	44	125
	% of respondents	14.4	50.4	35.2	100
6	Core sales and service branch – SSB	29	69	27	125
	% of respondents	23.2	55.2	21.6	100
7	Product and customer centric sales force	19	56	50	125
	% of respondents	15.2	44.8	40.0	100
8	Alternate delivery channels	5	59	61	125
	% of respondents	4.0	47.2	48.8	100

Source: Primary data

It is evident from the table that, 48.8% of the respondents are fully aware of alternate delivery channels,40% of the respondents have responded positively that they are fully aware of product and customer centric sales force.71.2% of the respondents are partly aware of Back-end software used for banking operations ,63.2% and 61.6% of the respondents are partly aware of Recommendations of Information technology in the banks and knowledge about electronic services offered by banks respectively. 38.4%, 23.2% and 20% of the respondents are not aware of Hardware knowledge to correct simple technical snags, Core sales and service branch - SSB's and Back-end software used for banking operations respectively. Thus we can conclude that the bank has to undertake training programs individually for each of the above aspects, separately so as to enable the employees to adopt themselves with the changes that have been made due to BPR initiatives at SBH.

The responses were quantified for further study by computing the weighted scores to find out aggregate level of awareness , these details are presented in table no 4.4.The following score have been assigned to quantify the responses: Fully Aware – 3, Partly Aware – 2, Not aware – 3.

Table No. 4.4

Employee's awareness on BPR initiatives at SBH

S.No.	Particulars	W.S	A.S	Rank
1	Back-end software used for banking operations	236	1.89	6
2	Recommendations of Information technology in the banks	274	2.19	5
3	Knowledge about electronic services offered by banks	290	2.32	2
4	Hardware knowledge to correct simple technical snags	217	1.74	7
5	Retail banking i.e. CPC's	276	2.21	4
6	Core sales and service branch - SSB	248	1.98	8
7	Product and customer centric sales force	281	2.25	3
8	Alternate delivery channels	306	2.45	1
	Total Score	**2128**	2.09	

Source : Primary data

It may be observed from the table that there is high level of awareness among the employees regarding BPR initiatives of the bank, with the aggregate score of 2.09 out of total 3. It is noticed that high level of awareness is found in case of alternate delivery channels (2.45), followed by knowledge about electronic services offered by the bank (2.32), product and customer centric sales force (2.25), retail banking (2.21), recommendations of information technology in banks (2.19). However the low awareness levels are found with respect to hardware knowledge to correct simple technical snags (1.74) and backend software used for banking operating (1.89).At the same time it is interesting to note that all the banking operations with BPR initiatives listed above are above average as they are above 1.5 out of 3 point scale.

Employee's awareness in relation to demographic variables: After identifying the awareness about BPR initiatives in banks as perceived by the employees, an attempt is made to find out whether there are any variations in responses of the employees based on age, gender, educational qualification, annual income, experience of the employees. For this purpose cross tabulation for the above variables is made and presented in tables 4.5 to 4.10

4.4 Age vs. Awareness of BPR requirements among the employees :

Awareness of BPR requirements among the employees are analyzed according to the age of the respondents and presented below :

Table No. 4.5

S.No.	Particulars	AGE					
		< 50 years			> 50 years		
		W.S	A.S	Rank	W.S	A.S	Rank
1	Back-end software used for banking operations	211	1.92	7	25	1.67	7.5
2	Recommendations of Information technology in the banks	244	2.21	5	30	2.0	5
3	Knowledge about electronic services offered by banks	258	2.35	2	32	2.13	2
4	Hardware knowledge to correct simple technical snags	192	1.75	8	25	1.67	7.5
5	Retail banking i.e. CPC's	244	2.22	4	32	2.13	2
6	Core sales and service branch - SSB	221	2.01	6	27	1.80	6
7	Product and customer centric sales force	249	2.26	3	32	2.13	2
8	Alternate delivery channels	275	2.50	1	39	2.07	4
	Total Score	1894	2.15		242	1.95	

Age vs. Awareness of BPR requirements among the employees

Source : Primary data

It is evident from the table that, respondents aged less than 50 years have a greater level of understanding with respect to alternate delivery channels, knowledge about electronic services offered by banks and product and customer centric sales force respectively. The respondents above 50 years are aware of electronic services offered by banks, retail banking i.e. CPC's and product and customer centric sales force. All the respondents irrespective of their age have low level of understanding with regards to back-end software used for banking operations and hardware knowledge to correct simple technical snags.

The chi – Square test values with regards to age and the awareness of various aspects stated in the table being .073,.252,.588,.718,.685,.174,.788 and .008. Since the values are more than .05 we can conclude that there is no significant relationship between age and awareness of the respondents, except for alternate delivery channels, where the respondents of more than 50 year are having a greater awareness, which is also reflected in their ranking in the table.

4.5 Gender vs. Awareness of BPR requirements among the employees :

Awareness of BPR requirements among the employees is classified and analyzed based on the gender of the respondents and presented below :

Table No. 4.6

Gender vs. Awareness of BPR requirements among the employees

S.No.	Particulars	Gender					
		Male			Female		
		W.S	A.S	Rank	W.S	A.S	Rank
1	Back-end software used for banking operations	145	1.84	7.5	91	1.98	8
2	Recommendations of Information technology in the banks	174	2.20	3	100	2.17	5
3	Knowledge about electronic services offered by banks	187	2.37	1.5	103	2.24	3.5
4	Hardware knowledge to correct simple technical snags	145	1.84	7.5	92	2.0	7
5	Retail banking i.e. CPC's	173	2.19	4	103	2.24	3.5
6	Core sales and service branch – SSB	152	1.92	6	96	2.09	6
7	Product and customer centric sales force	170	2.15	5	111	2.41	2
8	Alternate delivery channels	187	2.37	1.5	119	2.59	1
	Total Score	1333	2.11		815.00	2.22	

Source : Primary data

The above table clearly indicated that the male respondents have high level of awareness with regards to electronic services offered by banks and alternate delivery channels whereas female respondents have greater level of understanding with respect to alternate delivery channels and product and customer centric sales force. Both male and female respondents have very low level of awareness with regards to back-end software used for banking operations and hardware knowledge to correct simple technical snags. The chi square test values with regards to gender and awareness of the respondents to BPR initiatives are .307, .514, .429, .085, .651, .022, .132 and .086. Since the values are more than.05 we can conclude that there is a significant relationship between gender and awareness of the respondents, except for Core sales and service branch - SSB, where both the respondents have the same level of awareness, which is clearly seen in their ranking from the table.

4.6 Designation vs. Awareness of BPR requirements among the employees :

Awareness of BPR requirements among the employees is classified and analyzed based on the designation of the respondents and presented in table no 4.7.

Table No. 4.7

Designation vs. Awareness of BPR requirements among the employees

S.No.	Particulars	Designation					
		Asst. Manager			Branch Manager		
		W.S	A.S	Rank	W.S	A.S	Rank
1	Back-end software used for banking operation	146	1.87	7	90	1.91	5
2	Recommendations of Information technology in the banks	173	2.22	4	101	2.15	4
3	Knowledge about electronic services offered by banks	177	2.27	2.5	86	1.83	6.5
4	Hardware knowledge to correct simple technical snags	138	1.77	8	79	1.68	8
5	Retail banking i.e. CPC's	170	2.18	5	105	2.23	2
6	Core sales and service branch - SSB	162	2.08	6	86	1.83	6.5
7	Product and customer centric sales force	177	2.27	2.5	104	2.21	3
8	Alternate delivery channels	199	2.55	1	107	2.28	1
Total Score		1342	2.15		758	2.02	

Source : Primary data

From the table it is evident that both assistant manager and general managers have high level of awareness to alternate delivery channels. Next in the order of their priority we find that assistant managers have ranked electronic services offered by banks and Product and customer centric sales force have higher ranking. Whereas general managers have ranked 2 and 3 to retail banking i.e. CPC's and Product and customer centric sales force respectively.

In order to study the association between designation and awareness of the various factors chi-square values have been computed, which are as follows -.102, .471, .170, .024, .645,.129, .896, and .025. Since the values are more than .05 we can conclude that there is a significant relationship between designation and awareness of the respondents, except for hardware knowledge to correct simple technical snags and alternate delivery channels, where both the assistant managers and general managers have given the same ranking.

4.7 Experience vs. Awareness of BPR requirements among the employees :

Awareness of BPR requirements among the employees is classified and analysed based on the experience of the respondents and presented in table no 4.8

Table 4.8

Experience vs. Awareness of BPR requirements among the employees

S.No.	Particulars	Experience								
		< 5 years			5 - 10 years			> 10 years		
		W.S	A.S	Rank	W.S	A.S	Rank	W.S	A.S	Rank
1	Back-end software used for banking operations	67	1.91	7	74	2.11	7	26	2.36	1
2	Recommendations of Information techno-logy in the bank	74	2.11	5.5	26	2.36	4.5	174	2.20	4
3	Knowledge about electronic services offered by banks	78	2.23	4	28	2.55	2.5	184	2.33	2
4	Hardware know-ledge to correct simple technical snags	57	1.63	8	26	2.36	4.5	137	1.73	8
5	Retail banking i.e. CPC's	81	2.31	3	28	2.55	2.5	167	2.11	6
6	Core sales and service branch – SSB	74	2.11	5.5	23	2.09	8	151	1.91	7
7	Product and customer centric sales force	88	2.51	2	24	2.18	6	169	2.14	5
8	Alternate delivery channels	95	2.71	1	29	2.64	1	182	2.30	3
	Total Score	614	2.19		258	2.36		1190	2.14	

Source : Primary data

It is clear from the table that the respondents having less than 5 years of service have ranked alternate delivery channels, product and customer centric sales force and retail banking i.e. CPC's as the top three initiatives with high level of understanding. The respondents having 5 to 10 years of experience in order of priority have knowledge of electronic services offered by banks, retail banking i.e. CPC's and alternate delivery channels. The rest of the respondents having more than 10 years of experience have awareness high level of awareness with respect to Back-end software used for banking operations, electronic services offered by banks and alternate delivery channels.

The chi-square tests values are .988, .562, .457, .243, .100, .100, .324, .129, .008.Except for alternate delivery channels there is a significant relationship with the experience of the respondents and the level of awareness of BPR initiatives at SBH.

4.8 Annual Income vs. Awareness of BPR requirements among the employees:

Awareness of BPR requirements among the employees is classified and analysed based on the experience of the respondents and presented in table no 4.9.

Irrespective of income all the respondents have high level of awareness with regards to alternate delivery channels, where they have given highest score of 2.44 and 2.67 by the respondents with Rs. 5 lakhs per annum and an income of Rs. 5 to 10 lakhs per annum respectively. It is interesting to note that respondents with Rs. 5 lakhs per annum have given 3rd rank to product and customer centric sales force whereas the respondents with Rs. 5 to Rs. 10 lakhs per annum have a very low level of understanding to product and customer centric sales force as it is ranked seventh.

The chi - square values have been computed to study the relationship between annual income and awareness of the respondents. .537, .857, .944, .283, .738,.287, .329, .799 are the values which clearly indicates that there is no significant relationship between the two.

Table No. 4.9

Annual Income vs. Awareness of BPR requirements among the employees

S. No.	Particulars	Annual Income					
		<Rs. 5 lakhs			Rs. 5-10 lakhs		
		W.S	A.S	Rank	W.S	A.S	Rank
1	Back-end software used for banking operations	230	1.89	7	6	2	6.5
2	Recommendations of Information technology	267	2.19	5	7	2.33	3.5
3	Knowledge about electronic services offered by banks	283	2.32	2	7	2.33	3.5
4	Hardware knowledge to correct simple technical snags	210	1.72	8	7	2.33	3.5
5	Retail banking i.e. CPC's	269	2.20	4	7	2.33	3.5
6	Core sales and service branch – SSB	242	1.98	6	6	2.0	6.5
7	Product and customer centric sales force	276	2.26	3	5	1.67	7
8	Alternate delivery channels	298	2.44	1	8	2.67	1
	Total Score	2075	2.13		53	2.21	

Source : Primary data

4.9 Educational Qualification Vs. Awareness of BPR requirements among the employees :

Awareness of BPR requirements among the employees is classified and analysed based on the educational qualification of the respondents and presented in table no 4.10.

Table No. 4.10

S. No.	Particulars	Annual Income					
		<Rs. 5 lakhs			Rs. 5-10 lakhs		
		W.S	A.S	Rank	W.S	A.S	Rank
1	Back-end software used for banking operations	230	1.89	7	6	2	6.5
2	Recommendations of Information technology	267	2.19	5	7	2.33	3.5
3	Knowledge about electronic services offered by banks	283	2.32	2	7	2.33	3.5
4	Hardware knowledge to correct simple technical snags	210	1.72	8	7	2.33	3.5
5	Retail banking i.e. CPC's	269	2.20	4	7	2.33	3.5
6	Core sales and service branch - SSB	242	1.98	6	6	2.0	6.5
7	Product and customer centric sales force	276	2.26	3	5	1.67	7
8	Alternate delivery channels	298	2.44	1	8	2.67	1
Total Score		2075	2.13		53	2.21	

Source: Primary data

Educational Qualification vs. Awareness of BPR requirements among the employees

It is interesting to note from the table that an SSC qualified employee is having high level of awareness with regards to back-end software used for banking operations, as against the graduate and post graduate respondents who have given almost the least rank of 6th and 7th respectively. It is also found that there is greater level of awareness to alternate delivery channels.

4.10 BPR and its impact on job as perceived by employees

In order to understand employee's perception about the impact of BPR on the job related aspects, six statements have been developed to reflect their job aspects. The respondents were asked to indicate the degree of their agreement for each of the statements on a five point likert scale with responses- 1) strongly disagree, 2) disagree, 3) neither agree nor disagree, 4) agree and 5) strongly agree. Weights have been assigned as shown below.

Variables	Scores
Strongly Disagree	1
Disagree	2
Neither agree nor disagree	3
Agree	4
Strongly Agree	5

Weighted scores and average scores have been computed for the responses of the sample employees and presented in table no. 4.11

Table 4.11

BPR and its impact on employees

S.No.	Particulars	Weighted Score	Average Score	Rank
1	BPR in banks does not help to improve efficiency of employees.	277	2.22	5
2	It is difficult for the employees to switch over from manual system to computerized system.	288	2.30	4
3	Most of the bank employees took VRS on account of re-engineering of processes in banks	312	2.5	2
4	The bank employees are overburdened after BPR in banks.	305	2.44	3
5	We are losing face to face contact with customers an account of BPR in banks	366	2.93	1
6	There is a threat on status of employees due to BPR in the banks.	272	2.18	6
	Total	1820	2.43	

Source: Primary data

It may be observed from the table that the overall average score is 2.43 which is slightly less than the average of 2.5 on a five point scale. In spite of all the statements being negative, the BPR in banks is having a positive impact on the employees, where all the average scores of individual statements are below 2.5, except that they have a fear of losing face to face contact with customers. The least score of 2.18 is for threat on status of employees due to computerization in the banks, indicating that the employees have accepted the change and are in the process of adopting the same. At the same time since all the statements are negative, it may be interpreted that BPR in banks has low level of negative effect on the job related aspects of employees of SBH.

4.12 BPR and its impact on employees in relation to demographic variables :

Further efforts are being made to study the relationship of BPR and its impact on employees to that of demographic variables and presented in tables 4.12 to 4.17

4.12A Age vs. BPR and its impact on employees :

BPR and its impact on employees is classified according to the age of the respondents and presented below. All the respondents irrespective of their age have a fear of losing face to face contact of customers on account of BPR in banks. Respondents with less than 50 years believe that most of the bank employees took VRS on account of re-engineering of processes in banks. Whereas the respondents above 50 years feel that there is a threat on status of employees due to BPR in the banks.

The chi-square test values being greater than .05(.251, .729, .441, .667, .476 and.823,) clearly indicates that there is no association between the age of the respondents and the impact of BPR on the employees.

Table No. 4.12

Age vs. BPR and its impact on employees

S.No.	Particulars	AGE					
		< 50 years			> 50 years		
		W.S	A.S	Rank	W.S	A.S	Rank
1	BPR in banks does not help to improve efficiency of employees.	193	1.75	6	34	2.27	4
2	It is difficult for the employees to switch over from manual system to computerized system.	254	2.27	4	30	2.00	6
3	Most of the bank employees took VRS on account of re-engineering of processes in banks	279	2.52	2	33	2.20	5
4	The bank employees are overburdened after BPR in banks.	270	2.45	3	35	2.33	3
5	We are losing face to face contact with customers an account of BPR in banks	286	2.60	1	43	2.87	1
6	There is a threat on status of employees due to BPR in the banks.	233	2.12	5	39	2.60	2
Total Score		1709	2.29		226	2.38	

Source : Primary data

4.12B Designation vs. BPR and its impact on employees :

BPR and its impact on employees is classified according to the designation of the respondents and presented below :

Table No. 4.13

Designation vs. BPR and its impact on employees

S.No.	Particulars	Designation					
		Asst. Manager			Branch Manager		
		W.S	A.S	Rank	W.S	A.S	Rank
1	BPR in banks does not help to improve efficiency of employees.	122	1.56	6	105	2.23	5
2	It is difficult for the employees to switch over from manual system to computerized system.	187	2.40	3	101	2.15	6
3	Most of the bank employees took VRS on account of re-engineering of processes in banks	191	2.45	2	121	2.57	3
4	The bank employees are overburdened after BPR in banks.	182	2.33	4	123	2.62	2
5	We are losing face to face contact with customers an account of BPR in banks	196	2.51	1	134	2.85	1
6	There is a threat on status of employees due to BPR in the banks.	157	2.01	5	115	2.44	4
	Total Score	1035	2.21		699	2.48	

Source : Primary data

Both the respondents (assistant and branch managers) are of the opinion that BPR in banks will lead to losing face to face contact with customers. The assistant managers are of the opinion that most of the bank employees took VRS on account of re-engineering of processes in banks. But branch managers believe that the employees are overburdened after BPR in banks followed by the employees taking VRS. The average score of both assistant and branch managers are less than 2.5 out of 5 indicating that they have a positive impact of BPR in banks.

It is further studied that there is a significant relationship between designation of the respondents and the impact of BPR on factors such as "It is difficult for the employees to switch over from manual system to computerized system"," Most of the bank employees took VRS on account of re-engineering of processes in banks"," The bank employees are overburdened after BPR in banks" and" We are losing face to face contact with customers an account of BPR in banks" (412, .341, .217, and .243). There is no significant relationship between designation of the respondents and the two factors namely, "BPR in banks does not help to improve efficiency of employees", "There is a threat on status of employees due to BPR in the banks ", as the test values are less than .05(.014, .031).

4.12C Gender vs. BPR and its impact on employees :

BPR and its impact on employees is classified according to the gender of the respondents and presented below :

Table No. 4.14

Gender vs. BPR and its impact on employees

S.No.	Particulars	Gender					
		Male			Female		
		W.S	A.S	Rank	W.S	A.S	Rank
1	BPR in banks does not help to improve efficiency of employees.	153	1.94	6	74	1.61	6
2	It is difficult for the employees to switch over from manual system to computerized system.	162	2.05	5	126	2.74	1
3	Most of the bank employees took VRS on account of re-engineering of processes in banks	199	2.52	3	113	2.46	2
4	The bank employees are overburdened after BPR in banks.	215	2.72	2	90	1.96	4
5	We are losing face to face contact with customers an account of BPR in banks	216	2.73	1	98	2.13	3
6	There is a threat on status of employees due to BPR in the banks.	192	2.43	4	80	1.73	5
	Total Score	1137	2.4		581	2.11	

Source : Primary data

The average score of both male and female respondents are 2.4 and 2.11 respectively, (i.e. less than 2.5 out of 5), indicating that there is no negative impact on them with respect to BPR in banks, Both the respondent strongly believes that BPR in banks will improve the efficiency of the employees by assigning the least rank to BPR in banks does not help to improve efficiency of employees.

The chi-square test reveals that there is no association between gender and the impact of BPR on employees, as all the chi square test values are less than .05. (.010, .016, .002, .004, .000 and.025)

4.12D Annual Income vs. BPR and its impact on employees :

BPR and its impact on employees is classified according to the income of the respondents and presented below :

Table No. 4.15

Annual Income vs. BPR and its impact on employees

S.No.	Particulars	Annual Income					
		< Rs.5 lakhs			Rs.5 -10 lakhs		
		W. S	A.S	Rank	W. S	A.S	Rank
1	BPR in banks does not help to improve efficiency of employees.	224	1.84	6	3	1.0	6
2	It is difficult for the employees to switch over from manual system to computerized system.	252	2.07	4	5	1.67	4
3	Most of the bank employees took VRS on account of re-engineering of processes in banks	246	2.02	5	6	2.0	3
4	The bank employees are overburdened after BPR in banks.	301	2.47	2	4	1.33	5
5	We are losing face to face contact with customers an account of BPR in banks	316	2.59	1	14	4.6	1
6	There is a threat on status of employees due to BPR in the banks.	267	2.19	3	7	2.33	2
	Total Score	1606	2.2		39	2.16	

Source : Primary data

The above table clearly indicates that irrespective of annual income of the respondents, all of them have a fear of losing face to face contact with customers on account of BPR in banks as they have given the highest score for the same. At the same time both the respondent strongly disagree the statement that, BPR in banks does not help to improve efficiency of employees. Thus we find the positive impact of BPR on all the employees.

The chi-square test values are .714, .833, .148, .612, .007 and .016, thus we can conclude that there is an association between the income and the impact of BPR on employees, whereas there is no association between the income of the respondents and factors such as" We are losing face to face contact with customers an account of BPR in banks" and "a threat on status of employees due to BPR in the banks", as the values are less than .05.

4.12E Educational Qualification vs. BPR and its impact on employees :

BPR and its impact on employees is classified according to the educational qualification of the respondents and presented below :

Table No. 4.16

Educational qualification Vs. BPR and its impact on employees

S. No.	Particulars	Educational qualification								
		SSC & below			Graduation			Post graduation		
		W. S	A.S	Rank	W. S	A.S	Rank	W. S	A.S	Rank
1	BPR in banks does not help to improve efficiency of employees.	5	5	1	176	1.87	6	46	1.53	6
2	It is difficult for the employees to switch over from manual system to computerized system.	1	1	6	213	2.27	4	75	2.50	2
3	Most of the bank employees took VRS on account of reengineering of processes in banks	2	2	4.5	247	2.63	2	69	2.30	3
4	The bank employees are overburdened after BPR in banks.	3	3	3	236	2.51	3	66	2.20	4
5	We are losing face to face contact with customers an account of BPR in banks	2	2	4.5	252	2.68	1	76	2.53	1
6	There is a threat on status of employees due to BPR in the banks.	4	4	2	210	2.23	5	48	1.60	5
	Total Score	17	2.83		1334	2.37		380	2.11	

Source : Primary data

From the table respondent with SSC as the qualification strongly believes that BPR in banks does not help to improve efficiency of employees. Whereas the graduate and post graduate respondents totally disagree with the statement. Both graduates and post graduates have the fear of losing face to face contact with customers an account of BPR in banks and thus given the highest score. The respondent with SSC qualification believes that there is a threat on status of employees due to BPR in the banks.

Further the study finds that there is a significant relationship between educational qualification and the impact of BPR on employees. (.075, .524, .598, .153, .742 and .237.)

4.12F Experience vs. BPR and its impact on employees :

BPR and its impact on employees is classified according to the experience of the respondents and presented below. From the table below we find that the respondents having less than 5 years of experience strongly agree that "It is difficult for the employees to switch over from manual system to computerized system" as it is ranked 1st.It is totally contradicting to my personal belief, as I strongly felt that respondents with less than five years of experience belong to younger generation who are supposed to be well equipped with the latest technology. The respondents with 5 and above 10 years of experience are of the same opinion fearing to losing face to face contact with customers an account of BPR in banks and strongly disagree that, BPR in banks does not help to improve efficiency of employees. Thus the respondents with more than 5 years of experience have positive impact of BPR.

Table No. 4.17

Experience vs. BPR and its impact on employees

S. No.	Particulars	Experience								
		< 5 years			5 to 10 years			> 10 years		
		W. S	A.S	Rank	W. S	A.S	Rank	W. S	A.S	Rank
1	BPR in banks does not help to improve efficiency of employees.	54	1.54	6	16	1.45	6	157	1.99	6
2	It is difficult for the employees to switch over from manual system to computerized system.	104	2.97	1	25	2.27	3	159	2.01	5
3	Most of the bank employees took VRS on account of re-engineering of processes in banks	85	2.43	2	23	2.09	4	204	2.58	3
4	The bank employees are overburdened after BPR in banks.	75	2.14	3	22	2.0	5	207	2.62	2

5	We are losing face to face contact with customers an account of BPR in banks	64	1.83	4	26	2.36	1.5	240	3.04	1
6	There is a threat on status of employees due to BPR in the banks.	55	1.57	5	26	2.36	1.5	191	2.42	4
	Total Score	**437**	**2.08**		**138**	**2.09**		**1158**	**2.44**	

Source : Primary data

Further the study reveals that there is no significant relationship between the experience of the respondents and the impact of BPR on employees as the chi-square test values are .205, .001, .002, .021, .000 and .000.except for the first statement.

4.13 Benefits of BPR in banks – Employees perceptions

It is generally felt that the BPR in banks will benefit the employees in many ways, such as reduction in errors, increase in efficiency and time saving etc. In order to examine the perception s of employees about the benefits, they were asked to indicate the benefits in order of their preference by indicating ranks for the given benefits. Weights have been assigned to the ranks as follows :

Rank	Scores
1	10
2	9
3	8
4	7
5	6
6	5
7	4
8	3
9	2
10	1

Weighted scores and average scores have been computed and shown in table no 4.18

Table No. 4.18

Benefits of BPR in banks - employees perceptions

S.No.	Particulars	Weighted Score	Average Score	Rank
1	Faster customer service	977	7.82	1
2	Reduce transaction errors and misunderstandings	691	5.53	5
3	Lower transmission costs	744	5.95	4
4	Greater efficiency	860	6.88	3
5	Easy clearance	593	4.74	7
6	Time saving	917	7.34	2
7	Increase in the no of banking services	681	5.45	6
8	Retaining existing customers	541	4.33	8
9	Provides better management information	474	3.79	9
10	Increase in transaction volume	398	3.18	10
	. Total	6876	5.5	

Source : Primary data

It may be observed from the table that the average score is 5.5 on a 10 point scale indicating just the average score. The top most benefit as perceived by the bank employees is faster customer service 7.82, and the other benefits in order of their preference include time saving with the average score of 7.34,greater efficiency 6.88,lower transmission costs 5.95 , reduce of transaction errors and misunderstandings 5.53 etc.

4.14 Problems of BPR in banks - perceptions of bank employee

Having examined the responses of employees about the benefits of BPR, an attempt is made here to understand perception of employees about the problems faced on account of BPR in banks. For this purpose, they were given asked to indicate their preference for the problems encountered by them, by giving ranks to listed problems. Weights have been given for the ranks as shown below :

Rank	Scores
1	9
2	8
3	7
4	6
5	5
6	4
7	3
8	2
9	1

Weighted scores and average scores thus obtained are presented in table 4.19.

Table No. 4.19

Problems of BPR in banks – perceptions of bank employee

S.No.	Particulars	Weighted Score	Average Score	Rank
1	Lack of trained personnel	949	7.59	1
2	Loss of brain power	479	3.83	7
3	Security concern problems	703	5.62	3
4	Machine failures	910	7.28	2
5	Data integrity problems	691	5.53	4
6	Threat to status of employees	484	3.87	6
7	Threat to ego for employees	398	3.18	9
8	Threat to security for employees	423	3.38	8
9	Electricity disturbances	577	4.62	5
	Total	5614	4.99	

Source : Primary data

It may be observed from the table that the most important problem of BPR in banks as perceived by the employees is lack of trained personnel having the highest average score of 7.59 out of 9, thus indicating that the banks should train the personnel to increase their efficiency and to adopt themselves with the BPR initiatives in banks. Other problems in order of priority include machine failures, security concern problems, data integrity problems etc.

4.15 Level of satisfaction after BPR in banks - employees perceptions

The level of satisfaction on bank employees can be reflected on their level of satisfaction about their job after BPR in banks .In order to know the level of satisfaction for select job factors, they were asked to indicate their satisfaction on a five point scale with the responses – 1) highly satisfied, 2) satisfies, 3) neither satisfied nor dissatisfied, 4) dissatisfied and 5) highly dissatisfied.

Weights have been given for the responses as shown below :

Scale	Scale weights
Highly Satisfied	5
Satisfied	4
Neither satisfied nor dissatisfied	3
Dissatisfied	2
Highly dissatisfied	1

Weighted scores and average scores have been computed and shown in the following table no 4.20.

Table No. 4.20

Level of satisfaction of BPR in banks - Employees perception

S.No.	Particulars	Weighted Score	Average Score	Rank
1	Work load	420	3.36	4
2	Extra allowance	389	3.11	5
3	Recognition	457	3.66	2
4	Promotion opportunities	451	3.61	3
5	Salary and monetary benefits	383	3.06	6
6	Job security	490	3.92	1
	Total	**2590**	**3.45**	

Source : Primary data

It may be observed from the table that overall satisfaction among the listed factors is found to be 3.45 out of 5, which is far above the average level of satisfaction. Among the individual factors highest level of satisfaction was noticed in case of job security (3.92), followed by other factors such as recognition (3.66), promotion opportunities (3.61) and workload (3.36) etc.

4.16 Level of satisfaction among the employees vs. demographic variables

Further the study is made to know the association of these factors and its relationship with the various demographic variables. The data is tabulated, analyzed and presented in the following tables.

4.16A Age vs. Level of satisfaction of BPR at SBH

Level of satisfaction of BPR at SBH is also analyzed according to the age of the respondents and presented below :

Table No. 4.21

Age vs. Level of satisfaction of BPR at SBH

S.No.	Particulars	< 50 Years			> 50 Years		
		W.S	A.S	Rank	W.S	A.S	Rank
1	Work load	365	3.32	4	55	3.67	1
2	Extra allowance	339	3.08	5	50	3.33	5
3	Recognition	405	3.68	2	52	3.47	4
4	Promotion opportunities	398	3.62	3	53	3.53	3
5	Salary and monetary benefits	333	3.03	6	48	3.13	6
6	Job security	432	3.93	1	54	3.60	2
	Total	2272	3.44		312	3.46	

Source : Primary data

The respondents less than 50 years have highest level of satisfaction in security of the job, followed by recognition, promotional opportunities and workload. Whereas the respondents of more than 50 years have maximum satisfaction with respect to workload and followed by in the order of priority are job security, promotional opportunities and recognition. The overall average score of 3.44 and 3.46 for the respondents less than 50 years and more than 50 years respectively indicates that the employees have very high level of satisfaction of BPR at SBH.

The chi-square test values are .213, .592, .330, .064, .582 and .622, indicates that there is a significant relationship between age of the respondents and the level of satisfaction of BPR at SBH.

4.16B Designation vs. Level of satisfaction of BPR at SBH

Level of satisfaction of BPR at SBH is also analyzed according to the designation of the respondents and presented below :

Table No. 4.22

Designation vs. Level of satisfaction of BPR at SBH

S.No.	Particulars	Asst.Man			Gen.Man		
		W.S	A.S	Rank	W.S	A.S	Rank
1	Work load	281	3.60	4	129	2.74	5
2	Extra allowance	244	3.13	6	145	3.09	4
3	Recognition	289	3.71	2	168	3.57	3
4	Promotion opportunities	280	3.59	3	171	3.64	2
5	Salary and monetary benefits	263	3.37	5	128	2.72	6
6	Job security	312	4.0	1	178	3.79	1
Total		1669	3.57		919	3.26	

Source : Primary data

From the table it is evident that both assistant managers and general managers have high level of satisfaction with regards to the security of their job. Assistant managers have ranked the least as extra allowance, indicating low level of satisfaction, whereas the general managers have low level of satisfaction with respect to salary and monetary benefits.

There is an association between designation of the respondents and the level of satisfaction of the employees as the chi-square tests values are greater than .05 (.52, .184, .328, .177, .066 and .109).

4.16C Gender vs. Level of satisfaction of BPR at SBH

Level of satisfaction of BPR at SBH is also analyzed according to the gender of the respondents and presented below :

Table No. 4.23

Gender vs. Level of satisfaction of BPR at SBH

S.No	Particulars	Male			Female		
		W.S	A.S	Rank	W.S	A.S	Rank
1	Work load	252	3.19	4	168	3.65	4
2	Extra allowance	234	2.96	5	155	3.37	5
3	Recognition	286	3.62	3	171	3.72	2
4	Promotion opportunities	287	3.63	2	164	3.57	3
5	Salary and monetary benefits	236	2.99	6	147	3.20	6
6	Job security	293	3.71	1	197	4.28	1
Total		1588	3.35		1002	3.63	

Source : Primary data

Both male and female respondents have the highest level of satisfaction to job security as they have an average score of 3.71 and 4.28 out of 5. It is interesting to note that the ranking is almost the same except for recognition and promotion opportunities.

There is no association between gender of the respondents and the level of satisfaction of the employees with respect to extra allowance, promotion opportunities and job security as the chi-square tests values are less than .05 (.024, .006, .023).With respect to the remaining factors there is an association between the two as the test values are greater than .05.(131, .092,.116)

4.16D Annual Income vs. Level of satisfaction of BPR at SBH

Level of satisfaction of BPR at SBH is also analyzed according to the income levels of the respondents and presented below :

Table No. 4.24

Income vs. Level of satisfaction of BPR at SBH

S.No.	Particulars	< Rs. 5 Lakhs			> Rs. 5 Lakhs		
		W.S	A.S	Rank	W.S	A.S	Rank
1	Work load	408	3.34	4	12	4	3
2	Extra allowance	373	3.06	5	10	3.33	5.5
3	Recognition	445	3.65	2	12	4	3
4	Promotion opportunities	441	3.61	3	10	3.33	5.5
5	Salary and monetary benefits	371	3.04	6	12	4	3
6	Job security	477	3.91	1	13	4.33	1
Total		2515	3.44		69	3.83	

Source : Primary data

From the table it is evident that the respondents with annual income of less than Rs.5lakhs, have the highest level of satisfaction with job security followed by the order of priority recognition, promotional opportunities and workload. As against this the respondents having income of more than Rs 5 lakhs per annum apart from having greater satisfaction with their security of the job , the other factors in order of priority being workload, recognition and salary and monetary benefits.

It is found that the chi-square test values are greater than .05 (.055, .631, .631, .476, .436 and .932), therefore we can conclude that there is no significant difference between annual income of the respondents and the level of satisfaction of the employees.

4.16E Educational Qualification vs. Level of satisfaction of BPR at SBH

Level of satisfaction of BPR at SBH is also analyzed according to the educational qualifications of the respondents and presented below -

Table No. 4.25

Educational Qualification vs. Level of satisfaction of BPR at SBH

S.No.	Particulars	SSC & Below			Graduate			Post Graduate		
		W.S	A.S	Rank	W.S	A.S	Rank	W.S	A.S	Rank
1	Work load	4	4	2.5	318	3.38	4	98	3.27	4
2	Extra allowance	3	3	5	292	3.11	6	94	3.13	5
3	Recognition	2	2	6	342	3.64	2	113	3.77	2
4	Promotion opportunities	4	4	2.5	340	3.62	3	105	3.53	3
5	Salary and monetary benefits	4	4	2.5	298	3.17	5	81	2.70	6
6	Job security	4	4	2.5	348	3.70	1	121	4.03	1
	Total	21	3.5		1938	3.44		612	3.41	

Source : Primary data

The respondent with SSC as the educational qualification has the highest level of satisfaction equally with regards to workload, promotion opportunities, salary and monetary benefits and job security. Both graduates and post graduate respondents have maximum satisfaction with the security of their job. Graduate respondents have low level of satisfaction with extra allowance whereas post graduate respondents are not content with salary and monetary benefits.

There is an association between educational qualification of the respondents and the level of satisfaction of the employees as the chi-square test values are greater than .05. (.935, .694, .358, .715, .174 and .940).

4.16F Experience vs. Level of satisfaction of BPR at SBH

Level of satisfaction of BPR at SBH is also analyzed according to the experience of the respondents and presented below –

Table No. 4.26

Experience vs. Level of satisfaction of BPR at SBH

S.No.	Particulars	< 5 Years			5 to 10 Years			>10 Years		
		W.S	A.S	Rank	W.S	A.S	Rank	W.S	A.S	Rank
1	Work load	119	3.40	4	36	3.27	3.5	265	3.35	4
2	Extra allowance	113	3.23	5	31	2.82	6	245	3.10	5
3	Recognition	132	3.77	2	36	3.27	3.5	289	3.66	2
4	Promotion opportunities	128	3.66	3	39	3.55	2	284	3.59	3
5	Salary and monetary benefits	110	3.14	6	32	2.91	5	241	3.05	6
6	Job security	153	4.37	1	42	3.82	1	335	4.24	1
	Total	755	3.59		216	3.27		1659	3.5	

Source : Primary data

From the table above it is evident that all the respondents irrespective of their experience in the bank have almost the same level of satisfaction, starting with job security, promotional opportunities, workload and recognition. The aggregate average score being 3.59, 3.27 and 3.50 for the respondents having less than 5 years of experience, 5 to 10 years of experience and more than 10 years of experience respectively , indicates that the employees are highly satisfied and greatly motivated.

There is an association between experience and the level of satisfaction of the respondents, except for job security. The chi-square test values are .646, .552, .684, .172, .529 and .006.

4.17 Overall Impact of BPR in banks– employees perception

As the present study if focused to know the impact of BPR in banks on customers, employees and bank performance. An attempt is made to know the impact of BPR on these three categories from the view point of select bank employees. The responses have been arranged on five rating scale ranging 1) High Impact, 2) Moderate , 3) Little Impact, 4) No impact and 5) Adverse impact. Weights have been given as shown below:

Scale	Scale weights
High Impact	5
Moderate	4
Little Impact	3
No impact	2
Adverse impact	1

Weighted scores and average scores have been computed and shown in following table no 4.27

Table 4.27

Overall Impact of BPR in banks – employees perception

S.No.	Particulars	Weighted Score	Average Score
1	Customers	412	3.30
2	Employees	504	4.03
3	Bank Performance	540	4.32
	Total	1456	3.88

Source : Primary data

The aggregate level of impact is reflected on the average score being 3.88, indicating that there is a high level of impact of BPR in banks on, customers, employees and bank performance. The employees felt that the major impact of it is on bank performance (4.32) as indicated by both financial and operation indicators. In the opinion of sample respondents the impact of BPR in banks is relatively low on bank customers the as compared to bank performance and employees of the bank.

4.18 Employees perception of overall impact of BPR in relation to demographic variables :

Further the study is made to know the association if any with respect to overall impact of BPR and the demographic variables and presented in the following tables –

4.18A Age vs. Overall Impact of BPR in banks – employee's perception :

Overall Impact of BPR in banks is tabulated according to age of the respondents, analyzed and presented in the table below-

Table 4.28

Age vs. Overall Impact of BPR in banks - employee's perception

S. No.	Particulars	< 50 Years		> 50 Years	
		W.S	A.S	W.S	A.S
1	Customers	461	4.19	62	4.13
2	Employees	446	4.05	58	3.87
3	Bank Performance	485	4.41	64	4.27
Total		1392	4.22	184	4.09

Source : Primary data

It is evident from the table above that the respondents, less than 50 years and above 50 years , perceive that the overall impact is first on bank performance, followed by on customers and then on employees.

There is an association between the age of the respondents and the overall impact of BPR at SBH (.877, .727, .317.).

4.18B Designation vs. Overall Impact of BPR in banks - employee's perception:

Overall Impact of BPR in banks is tabulated according to designation of the respondents, analyzed and presented in the table below :

Table 4.29

Designation vs. Overall Impact of BPR in banks - employee's perception

S. No.	Particulars	Asst. Man.		Gen. Man.	
		Weighted Score	Average Score	Weighted Score	Average Score
1	Customers	342	4.38	191	4.06
2	Employees	320	4.10	184	3.91
3	Bank Performance	348	4.46	201	4.28
Total		1010	4.31	576	4.08

Source : Primary data

The respondents i.e. branch managers and assistant managers responded the same, they are of the opinion that the impact of BPR is seen first on bank performance, then on customers and the last on employees.

Further we can conclude that there is an association between the designation of the respondents and the overall impact of BPR on customers and on employees. At the same time we find no association between designation of the respondents and overall impact of BPR on bank performance (.107,.065and.041).

4.18C Gender vs. Overall Impact of BPR in banks – employee's perception :

Overall Impact of BPR in banks is tabulated according to gender of the respondents, analyzed and presented in the table below :

Table 4.30

Gender vs. Impact of BPR in banks – employee's perception

S. No.	Particulars	Male		Female	
		Weighted Score	Average Score	Weighted Score	Average Score
1	Customers	337	4.27	193	4.20
2	Employees	316	4.00	188	4.09
3	Bank Performance	350	4.43	199	4.33
Total		1003	4.23	580	4.21

Source : Primary data

From the above table it is evident that both the male and female respondents feel that the overall impact of BPR in banks is first felt from bank performance, followed by on customers and employees.

There is no association between gender of the respondent and the overall impact of BPR on customers (.019).We also find a significant relationship between gender and the impact on employees and bank performance (.533, .267).

4.18D Annual Income vs. Overall Impact of BPR in banks – employee's perception:

Overall Impact of BPR in banks is tabulated according to the income levels of the respondents, analyzed and presented in the table below :

Table 4.31

Income vs. Overall Impact of BPR in banks – employee's perception

S.No.	Particulars	< Rs. 5 Lakhs		> Rs. 5 Lakhs	
		Weighted Score	Average Score	Weighted Score	Average Score
1	Customers	520	4.26	13	4.33
2	Employees	489	4.01	15	5
3	Bank Performance	489	4.01	15	5
	Total	1498	4.09	43	4.78

Source : Primary data

Respondents having an annual income of less than Rs.5 lakhs perceive differently, as we find that they are of the opinion that the impact is more on customers followed by bank performance and employees. Whereas respondents having above Rs.5 lakhs income feel that the impact is more on bank performance and employees.

There is a significant relationship between the annual income of the respondents and the overall impact of BPR on customers, employees and on bank performance (.891, .063, .344).

4.18E Experience vs. Overall Impact of BPR in banks – employee's perception:

Overall Impact of BPR in banks is tabulated according to the experience of the respondents, analyzed and presented in the table below :

Table 4.32

Experience Vs. Overall Impact of BPR in banks – employee's perception

S.No.	Particulars	< 5 Years		5 to 10 Years		> 10 Years	
		Weighted Score	Average Score	Weighted Score	Average Score	Weighted Score	Average Score
1	Customers	149	4.26	46	4.18	338	4.28
2	Employees	145	4.14	45	4.09	314	3.97
3	Bank Performance	151	4.31	51	4.64	347	4.39
	Total	445	4.24	142	4.3	999	4.21

Source : Primary data

Irrespective of the experience of the respondents we find that all the respondents have the same view with respect to overall impact of BPR. The respondents are of the view that the impact in order of priority being bank performance followed by customers and employees.

There is no association with respect to experience of the respondents and the overall impact of BPR on customers (.026). Further the study reveals that there an association between experience of the respondents and overall impact of BPR on employees and on bank performance (.569, .347).

4.18F Educational qualification vs. Overall Impact of BPR in banks – employee's perception :

Overall Impact of BPR in banks is tabulated according to the educational qualification of the respondents, analyzed and presented in the table below :

Table 4.33

Educational Qualification vs. Overall Impact of BPR in banks – employee's perception

S.No.	Particulars	SSC & Below		Graduate		Post Graduate	
		Weighted Score	Average Score	Weighted Score	Average Score	Weighted Score	Average Score
1	Customers	5	5	396	4.21	129	4.30
2	Employees	5	5	374	3.98	125	4.17
3	Bank Performance	4	4	411	4.37	134	4.47
	Total	14	4.67	1181	4.19	388	4.31

Source : Primary data

It is evident from the above table that, the respondents with SSC as the educational qualification opined that the overall impact is more on customers and employees. But both graduate and post graduate respondents are of the opinion that the overall impact is more on bank performance followed by customers.

We can conclude that there is an association between educational qualification of the respondents and overall impact of BPR on customers, on employees and on bank performance (.577, .736, .712).

4.19 The level of satisfaction of employees about banking services after BPR at SBH

Since bank employees are highly involved in handling different bank services, an attempt is made to elicit their vies in identifying the services which are highly improved due to BPR in banks. For this purpose the respondents were asked to indicate their satisfaction of the various banking services on a five point scale with the responses, 1) Highly Satisfied, 2) Satisfies, 3) Neither satisfied nor dissatisfied, 4) Dissatisfied and 5) Highly dissatisfied.

Weights have been given for the responses as shown below :

Scale	Scale weights
Highly Satisfied	5
Satisfied	4
Neither satisfied nor dissatisfied	3
Dissatisfied	2
Highly dissatisfied	1

Weighted scores and average scores have been computed and shown in the following table no 4.34

Table No. 4.34

Level of satisfaction of employees about banking services after BPR at SBH

S. No.	Particulars	Weighted Score	Average Score	Rank
1	Cash payments	537	4.32	4
2	Cash receipts	532	4.26	6
3	Printed statements of various accounts	552	4.42	2
4	Issue of cheque book	529	4.23	8.5
5	Issue of drafts	539	4.31	5
6	Fund transfer	566	4.53	1
7	Disbursement of loans	484	3.87	12
8	Multi – service on a single counter	525	4.20	10
9	ATM cum Debit card facilities	530	4.24	7
10	Credit card management	487	3.90	11
11	Internet banking	544	4.35	3
12	Drop boxes	529	4.23	8.5
	Total	6354	4.24	

Source : Primary data

It may be observed from the table that the employees are highly satisfied about improvement of all services provided after BPR. The highest level of satisfaction in order of priority is indicated in case of "Fund transfer", "Printed statements of various accounts", "Internet banking", "Cash payments" and "Issue of drafts".

4.20 Improvement in customers services after BPR in banks – employees perceptions :

Scale	Scores
Good	3
Average	2
Poor	1

The SBH has implemented BPR with the objectives such as - Simplify customer facing branch processes, Migrate non-customer facing processes to central processing centres, Empower branches to become sales, service and marketing units, Raise customer satisfaction levels, to enhance productivity and to connect with the customer and cement the relationships. It is generally felt that there is significant improvement in customer services after BPR as compared to the period before BPR. Hence, an attempt is made to examine the responses of employees on improvement of customer services after BPR in banks. The employees were asked to indicate their responses on three point scale with responses: 1) good, 2) average and 3) poor. The weights have been assigned as under –

The weighted scores and average scores have been computed and shown in the following table no 4.35

Table No. 4.35

Improvement in customer services before and after BPR - Employees perceptions

S.No.	Transaction	Before 2005		After 2005		Diff. in A.S	Rank
		W.S	A.S	W.S	A.S		
1	Cash withdrawal	248	1.98	344	2.75	0.77	8
2	Deposit of cash	254	2.03	353	2.82	0.79	7
3	Opening a new account	225	1.8	340	2.72	0.92	5
4	Obtaining demand draft or pay order	254	2.03	358	2.86	0.83	6
5	Updating the pass book	218	1.74	358	2.86	1.12	4

6	Calculation of product interest on the balance	219	1.75	365	2.92	1.17	3
7	Clearance of outstation cheques/ DD's	311	2.49	360	2.88	0.39	9
8	Inter branch reconciliation	207	1.66	375	3.0	1.34	1
9	Furnishing of bank statements to the customers	216	1.73	368	2.94	1.21	2
	Total Scores	**2152**	**17.21**	**3221**	**25.75**	**8.54**	
	Average Scores	**1.91**		**2.86**		**.95**	

Source : Primary data

It may be observed from the table that there has been significant improvement in customers services after BPR as perceived by the employees of SBH. The significant improvement is found in order of ranking, for "inter branch reconciliation", "furnishing of bank statements to the customers", "calculation of product interest on the balance", "updating the pass book", "opening a new account" etc.

Some of the personnel feeling of the respondents are stated below :

"In the changing scenario of LPG and greater demand for customers services , BPR for the banks is inevitable"

"Though the BPR has initiated it has not been properly implemented ,required things has not been provided"

"BPR initiative is a well thought entry in the banking sector in terms of customer satisfaction, for employees and for bank".

"The tremendous competition in banking industry or delay in processing requests and burden of work on employee has increased a lot. "

"Better customer service provided in lesser time and resulting in more productivity of the employees".

"BPR initiative is technically though sound but manpower is less ,so taking time in processing would be faster if more processing officers are employed".

"Customers are slightly unhappy due to lack of trained personal at the front end. So we are unable to give the best services in some aspects due to non initiative in implementing new technology".

"After computerization staffs are overburden, stress has been more".

"All are very happy with the changes in banking sector. We want to improve and facilitate the customers".

"Due to ATM machine failures many complaints are coming and due to network connectivity customers feel dissatisfied with our service."

"BPR initiatives have totally changed the face of the bank from traditional banking to a world class bank."

"Customers are not able to accept some of the initiatives like drop boxes and CPC'S there is lot of queries and delay regarding loan processing".

"With BPR initiative I am satisfied because of low risk .Internet Banking and ATM customer crowds are less as compared to earlier".

"Customers are benefitted with better service"

"With the technological initiatives of BPR we are in comfortable working atmosphere and the customers are getting faster customer service. I am personally happy with BPR initiatives and welcome the new developments in the future".

Implementation of BPR initiatives in the bank is not yet complete and now the bank is facing lot of teething problems, According to him it is only 40% of the work that is completed.

Thus the study reveals that the impact of BPR on employees is positive as perceived by the sample respondents. There is high-level of understanding among the employees about the various BPR initiatives taken up by their bank except for back-end software used for banking operations and hardware knowledge to correct simple technical snags. The major problems faced by the sample respondents being lack of trained personnel and machine failures. It is found that the sample respondents perceive the impact of BPR more on bank performance as compared to its impact on customers and employees. Though majority of banking services witnessed improvement after BPR, the sample respondents are of the opinion that some of the services can be improved further namely clearance of outstation cheques, deposit and withdrawal of cash.

The following conclusions were drawn :

1. The employees considered speedy operations with a maximum average score of 8.55 as the major objective of BPR in banks. In the order of priority the other objectives include, better customer services (8.43), adoption of latest technology (7.42), accuracy of transactions (7.10) and cost reduction in operations (6.93).to satisfy existing customers (5.55) and to create new customers (5.31) and the least importance is given to easy rectification of errors and reduction of staff.

2. It is found that, 48.8% of the respondents are fully aware of alternate delivery channels,40% of the respondents have responded positively that they are fully aware of product and customer centric sales force.71.2% of the respondents are partly aware of Back-end software used for banking operations ,63.2% and 61.6% of the respondents are partly aware of Recommendations of Information technology in the banks and knowledge about electronic services offered by banks respectively. 38.4%, 23.2% and 20% of the respondents are not aware of Hardware knowledge to correct simple technical snags, Core sales and service branch – SSB's and Back-end software used for banking operations respectively.

3. It was found that there is high level of awareness among the employees regarding BPR initiatives of the bank, with the aggregate score of 2.09 out of total 3. It is noticed that high level of awareness is found in case of alternate delivery channels (2.45), knowledge about electronic services offered by the bank (2.32), product and customer centric sales force (2.25), retail banking (2.21), recommendations of information technology in banks (2.19).

4. There is also the low awareness levels found with respect to hardware knowledge to correct simple technical snags (1.74) and backend software used for banking operating (1.89).

5. It is found that the BPR in banks is having a positive impact on the employees, where all the average scores of individual statements are below 2.5out of 5,as the statements given were negative except that they have a fear of losing face to face contact with customers. The least score of 2.18 is for threat on status of employees due to computerization in the banks, indicating that the employees have accepted the change and are in the process of adopting the same.

6. It is found that the average score is 5.5 on a 10 point scale indicating just the average score. The top most benefit as perceived by the bank employees is faster customer service 7.82, and the other benefits in order of their preference include time saving with the average score of 7.34,greater efficiency 6.88,lower transmission costs 5.95 , reduce of transaction errors and misunderstandings 5.53 etc.

7. It can be concluded that the most important problem of BPR in banks as perceived by the employees is lack of trained personnel having the highest average score of 7.59 out of 9.

8. It is found that overall satisfaction among the listed factors is 3.45 out of 5, which is far above the average level of satisfaction. Among the individual factors highest level of satisfaction was noticed in case of job security (3.92), followed by other factors such as recognition (3.66), promotion opportunities (3.61) and workload (3.36) etc.

9. It is found that there is a high level of impact of BPR in banks on, customers, employees and bank performance. The employees felt that the major impact of it is on bank performance (4.32) as indicated by both financial and operation indicators. In the opinion of sample respondents the impact of BPR in banks is relatively low on bank customers as compared to bank performance and employees of the bank.

10. It can be concluded that the employees are highly satisfied about improvement of all banking services provided after BPR. The highest level of satisfaction in order of priority is indicated in case of "Fund transfer", "Printed statements of various accounts ", "Internet banking", "Cash payments" and "Issue of drafts".

11. It is found that there has been significant improvement in customers services after BPR as perceived by the employees of SBH. The significant improvement is found in order of ranking, for "inter branch reconciliation", "furnishing of bank statements to the customers", "calculation of product interest on the balance", "updating the pass book", "opening a new account" etc.

II To find out the impact of Business process Re- Engineering, on Employees of State Bank of Hyderabad,the following hypotheses were formulated and tested.

Hypotheses 4

The awareness of the BPR initiatives among the employees of SBH is independent of the demographic variables of the respondent.

a) we can conclude that there is a significant relationship between age and awareness of the respondents with respect to back-end software used for banking operations, recommendations of Information technology in the banks, knowledge about electronic services offered by banks, hardware knowledge to correct simple technical snags, retail banking i.e. CPC's, Core sales and service branch - SSB, and Product and customer centric sales force. At the same time the study reveals that there is no association between the age of the respondents and the awareness of alternate delivery channels.

b) We can conclude that there is a significant relationship between gender of the respondents and awareness of the respondents, except for Core sales and service branch - SSB, where both the respondents have the same level of awareness, which is clearly seen in their ranking from the table.

c) We can conclude that there is a significant relationship between designation of the respondents and awareness of the respondents, except for hardware knowledge to correct simple technical snags and alternate delivery channels, where both the assistant managers and general managers have given the same ranking.

d) Further we conclude that, except for alternate delivery channels there is a significant relationship with the experience of the respondents and the level of awareness of BPR initiatives at SBH.

e) There is a significant relationship between the income of the respondents and the awareness of BPR initiatives.

Hypotheses 5

The level of job satisfaction of the employees at SBH is independent of the demographic variables of the respondent.

The above hypotheses is tested and the following conclusion derived as follows :

a. The study indicates that there is a significant relationship between age of the respondents and the level of satisfaction of BPR at SBH.

b. There is an association between designation of the respondents and the level of satisfaction of the employees at SBH.

c. There is no association between gender of the respondents and the level of satisfaction of the employees with respect to extra allowance, promotion opportunities and job security as the chi-square tests values are less than .05 (.024, .006, .023).With respect to the remaining factors there is an association between the two as the test values are greater than .05.(131, .092,.116)

d. We can conclude that there is no significant difference between annual income of the respondents and the level of satisfaction of the employees.

e. There is an association between educational qualification of the respondents and the level of satisfaction of the employees.

f. There is an association between experience of the respondents and the level of satisfaction of the respondents, except for job security.

Hypotheses 6

BPR and its impact on employees are independent of the demographic variables of the respondent.

The hypotheses is tested and the following conclusions derived –

a. The study clearly indicates that there is no association between the age of the respondents and the impact of BPR on the employees.

b. It is further studied that there is a significant relationship between designation of the respondents and the impact of BPR on factors such as "It is difficult for the employees to switch over from manual system to computerized system"," Most of the bank employees took VRS on account of re-engineering of processes in banks"," The bank employees are overburdened after BPR in banks" and" We are losing face to face contact with customers an account of BPR in banks" (412, .341, .217, and .243). There is no significant relationship between designation of the respondents and the two factors namely, "BPR in banks does not help to improve efficiency of employees", "There is a threat on status of employees due to BPR in the banks ", as the test values are less than .05(.014, .031).

c. We find that there is no association between gender and the impact of BPR on employees,

d. We can conclude that there is an association between the income of the respondents and the impact of BPR on employees. It is also found that there is no association between the income of the respondents and factors such as" We are losing face to face contact with customers an account of BPR in banks" and "a threat on status of employees due to BPR in the banks".

e. Further the study finds that there is a significant relationship between educational qualification and the impact of BPR on employees.

f. There is no significant relationship between the experience of the respondents and the impact of BPR on employees

Hypotheses 7

The overall impact of BPR at SBH is independent of the demographic variables of the respondent.

The above hypotheses were tested and the following results derived:

a. There is an association between the age of the respondents and the overall impact of BPR at SBH

b. Further we can conclude that there is an association between the designation of the respondents and the overall impact of BPR on customers and on employees. At the same time we find no association between designation of the respondents and overall impact of BPR on bank performance (.107,.065and.041).

c. There is no association between gender of the respondent and the overall impact of BPR on customers (.019).We also find a significant relationship between gender and the impact on employees and bank performance (.533, .267).

d. There is a significant relationship between the annual income of the respondents and the overall impact of BPR on customers, employees and on bank performance (.891, .063, .344).

e. There is no association with respect to experience of the respondents and the overall impact of BPR on customers (.026). Further the study reveals that there an association between experience of the respondents and overall impact of BPR on employees and on bank performance (.569, .347).

f. We can conclude that there is an association between educational qualification of the respondents and overall impact of BPR on customers, on employees and on bank performance (.577, .736, .712).

Suggestions :

- Awareness among all the employees i.e. (different cadres working in the bank) should be created relating to the various initiatives taken up by the bank.
- Any change made in the bank should also result in the change in attitude of the employees. Management should take the necessary action and try to involve all the employees do the same.
- The bank has to undertake training programs individually for each of the BPR initiatives, separately so as to enable the employees to adopt themselves with the changes that have been made in SBH.
- As the sample respondents feel that the impact of BPR is found more on bank performance as compared to employees, the management should consider the same and try to also include productivity based pay scale in addition to the regular pay.
- Efforts should be made to make arrangements for continuous power supply and minimum of machine failures to avoid inconvenience to employees and customers.

❖ ❖ ❖

CHAPTER - V

Impact of BPR at SBH on Customers - Analysis of Customers Perceptions

5.1 Introduction

Customers have always been at the center stage of any business organization. Customer satisfaction is the strongest foundation for the success of an organization. An organization cannot survive in the long run if its customers are dissatisfied with the products or the services offered by it. Markets are driven by the forces of demand and supply, and in the wake of liberal import policies and open doors for foreign investment the market scenario of business has turned from that of "sellers market" to "buyers market". The growing expectations of the customers, fast changing preference and opportunities available to him as consumer have made him the king in the true sense. Retaining old customers and winning new ones is proving to be a tough challenge. As a result customer's satisfaction is a growing concern for the organizations that want to grow in this competitive world. Customer satisfaction has been defined in several ways. Most important of them being: Expectations Performance & Interactions, Pleasure/Displeasure and the Evaluation of the Benefits of Consumptions. It has also been defined as the degree of happiness a customer experiences with the services provided by the banks.

There are two main theories explaining the same :

Assimilation Theory :

According to this customers do not easily accept discrepancy from their pre - conceived notions and beliefs. Moreover in case of discrepancy they tend to minimize the discrepancy between expectations and the product performance by adjusting their perceptions of the performance to be more consistent with their expectations. As a result the satisfaction judgment of an expectation oriented customer is likely to be similar to the emotions surrounding his/her expectations.

Contrast Effect Theory :

According to this the customers magnify or exaggerate the difference between their expectations and product performance in the direction of disconfirmation. During positive disconfirmation they rate the product performance is higher than what they would have rated if they had no prior expectations. In negative disconfirmation, they rate the product performance lower than what it would have been in absence of any prior expectations. This results in higher levels of customer satisfaction when their expectations are low and lower level customer satisfaction when their expectations are high.

The purpose of the present chapter is to explain and analyze the views of sample customers about the impact of BPR on performance of selected branches of SBH. Apart from direct interviews with the customers of the bank, a structured questionnaire was executed to know the perceptions of the consumers in relation to Business Process Reengineering in banks focussing on issues relating to :

1) Objectives of BPR in banks i.e. vis a vis customer perception.
2) Purpose of visiting the bank and the frequency of visits by the consumers.
3) Time spent by the customers while transacting with the bank before and after BPR.
4) Awareness and usage of various services by the consumers.
5) Customers level of satisfaction of BPR initiatives at SBH.
6) BPR's impact on customers, employees and bank as perceived by customers.
7) Benefits of BPR to the customers
8) Problems faced by them due to BPR.

For the convenience of the discussion the chapter is divided into two parts (i.e. Part A and Part B). Part 'A' covers a brief profile of sample customers. While Part 'B' presents the responses of the respondents regarding, the impact of BPR on customer satisfaction at SBH.

5.2 Profile of Sample Customers

Table – 5.1

Profile of Sample Customers

S.No.	Demographic Variables	Classification	Frequency	Percentage
1	AGE	< 25 yrs	26	10.4
		25-50 yrs	104	41.6
		Above 50 yrs	120	48.0
		Total	250	100.0
2	Sex	Male	182	72.8
		Female	68	27.2
		Total	250	100.0

3	Computer skills	Yes	134	53.6
		No	116	46.4
		Total	250	100.0
4	Occupation	Business	33	13.2
		Employment	144	57.6
		Others	73	29.2
		Total	250	100.0
5	Annual Income	Less than Rs. 5 lakhs	172	68.8
		Rs.5 lakhs to Rs.10 lakhs	70	28.0
		Above Rs10 lakhs	8	3.2
		Total	250	100.0

The details of profile in table No. 4.1 are discussed below :

1. It may be observed from the table that 10.4% of the respondents are below 25 years of age, 41.6% are in the age group of 25 to 50 years and 48% of the respondents are above 50 years. Thus major parts of the sample are middle and old aged persons.

2. With regards to sex composition of the respondents 72.8% of them are male and 27.2% are females.

3. Majority of the respondents' i.e.53.6% of the respondents are computer literates and almost an equal percentage of the respondents (46.4%) have no knowledge of computer skills.

4. Only 13.2% of the respondents are having their own business, more than half of the respondents are employees' i.e.57.6% and 29.2% of the sample population belong to student and other categories.

5. Income wise analysis shows that 68.8% of them are in the income group of less than Rs.5 lakhs, 28% of them are in the group of Rs.5 lakhs to Rs. 10 lakhs and the rest only 3.2% of the respondents belong to annual income of Rs.10 lakhs and above.

6. 90% of the sample customers are having savings accounts in the bank and only 10% of them are current account holders.

7. Only 10.8% of the respondents are having educational qualification SSC and below, 51%of the respondents are graduates and the rest (37.8%) are post graduates and above.

Thus the major parts of the respondents are in the age groups of above 25 years and above, almost three – fourth of the respondents are males, most of them are in the income group of less than Rs. 5 Lakhs per annum, 90% of the respondents are saving account holders and 60% of them are employees.

PART B

5.3 CUSTOMER PERCEPTIONS

In this chapter an attempt is made to discuss the opinions of SBH customers on various relevant issues on Business process Re-Engineering at SBH and its impact on the customer satisfaction. The issues examined include how customers perceive the objectives of BPR in banks, purpose of visiting the bank, frequency of visiting the bank, time taken for various transactions before and after BPR, awareness and usage of BPR services provided by banks, satisfaction about the banking services after BPR, benefits of BPR at SBH, problems faced by the customers after BPR in the bank, impact of BPR on customers, employees and bank performance.

5.4 Customer's perceptions – on objectives of BPR

In order to understand the objectives of BPR at SBH from the point of view of customers, an attempt was made to collect their responses about major objectives of BPR in commercial banks. The objectives indicated by them have been grouped into eight categories and their responses are shown in table no. 5.2

Table 5.2

Objectives of BPR – Customers Perceptions

S.No	Variables	No of respondents	%
1	Anywhere banking	176	17
2	Faster and efficient customer service	211	20
3	To enhance quality of customer service	103	10
4	Reducing the operational cost	97	9
5	Offering multiple delivery channels	78	8
6	Centralizing the bank end processes	73	7
7	Creating a customer profile database	54	9
8	Speedy operations	146	14
9	To create new customer	91	9
	Total	1029	100

Source : Primary data

It may be observed from the table that customers perceived "Better Customer Service (20%)" as the primary objective of BPR in banks followed by, "Anywhere banking (17%)", and speedy operations (14%)" as few other major objectives of BPR in banks. Other objectives in order of priority include - Reducing the operational cost, creating a customer profile database to create new customer, offering multiple delivery channels, Centralizing the bank end processes.

5.5 Purpose of visit to the banks

The impact of BPR of banking services on customers is influenced by the purpose for which the customers are visiting the bank. In order to know customer's purpose in visiting the banks the sample respondents were asked to indicate their responses. These responses have been analysed and presented in table 5.3

Table 5.3

Purpose of visit to the bank

S. No.	Particulars	Rank 1	Rank 2	Rank 3	Rank 4	Rank 5	Rank 6	Rank 7
1	Deposit / Withdrawal of cash	177	29	24	11	5	-	4
	% of Respondents	**71**	12	10	4	2	-	2
2	Demand draft / Pay order	14	76	49	6	28	2	18
	% of Respondents	6	**30**	**20**	25	11	1	7
3	Credit Card Transactions	11	18	48	54	49	52	18
	% of Respondents	4	7	19	22	20	21	7
4	Updating the Pass book	33	89	49	41	13	16	9
	% of Respondents	13	**36**	20	16	5	6	4
5	Cash credit Operations	3	6	13	22	82	84	40
	% of Respondents	1	2	5	9	**33**	**34**	16
6	Locker facilities	6	17	45	33	47	61	41
	% of Respondents	2	7	18	13	19	**24**	**16**
7	Availing Loan services	5	15	26	32	28	29	115
	% of Respondents	2	6	10	13	11	12	**46**

Source : Primary data

It may be observed from the above table that 71% of the respondents are primarily visiting the bank for deposit and withdrawal of cash. At the same time we find that the respondents have allotted first three ranks to this service whereby we can conclude that more than 90% of the customers visit the banks for deposit and withdrawal of cash. 46% of the customers visit the bank for availing loan facilities, followed by 67% (33% plus 34%) of the respondents visit the bank for cash credit operations, around 36% of the customers visit the bank for updating the pass books and 50% (30%+20%)of the respondents visit the bank for obtaining demand drafts and pay orders.

5.6 Frequency of visiting the bank

Availing the banking services also depends on the frequency of visiting the bank by the customers.BPR in banks enables them in speedy operations, resulting in reduction of time while providing services to customers. Here an attempt is made to examine customers practices regarding frequency of visit to bank to avail services, figures are shown in table No. 5.4

Table No. 5.4

Frequency of Visit to the Bank

S.No.	Particulars	Frequency	Percent
1	Daily	31	12.4
2	Once in a week	91	36.4
3	Once in a month	107	42.8
4	Once in three months	21	8.4
	Total	250	100.0

Source : Primary data

It may be observed from the table that most of the customers (42.8%) visit once in a month, followed by once in a week (36.4%), and daily (12.4%).

5.5 Demographic variables of the respondents vs. customer perceptions about frequency of visit to the bank

After identifying the frequency of visits to the bank by the customers, an attempt is made to find out whether there are any variations in responses of the customers based on demographic variable such as age, sex, income computer skills and occupation. The responses are analysed and shown in table no 5.5.

Table No 5.5

Demographic Variables vs. Frequency of Visit to the (%)

S. No.	Variables	Particulars	Daily	Once a week	once in a month	Once in three months	Total	Chi-Square Test
1	Age Wise	< 25 yrs	2.4	1.6	5.2	1.2	10.4	.075
		25-50 yrs	7.2	16.4	13.2	4.8	41.6	
		Above 50 yrs	2.8	18.4	24.4	2.4	48	
		Total	12.4	36.4	42.8	8.4	100	
2	Sex wise	Male	8.4	30.8	29.6	4.0	72.8	.090
		Female	4	5.6	13.2	4.4	27.2	
		Total	12.4	36.4	42.8	8.4	100	
3	Computer Skills	Yes	6.8	19.6	24.0	3.2	53.6	.085
		No	5.6	16.8	18.8	5.2	46.4	
		Total	12.4	36.4	42.8	8.4	100	
4	Occupation	Business	3.6	7.2	2.4	0	13.2	.011
		Employment	5.6	21.6	22.8	7.6	57.6	
		Others	3.2	7.6	17.6	0.8	29.2	
		Total	12.4	36.4	42.8	8.4	100	
5	Income	< Rs. 5 lakhs	7.6	28.4	27.6	5.2	68.8	.311
		Rs..5 to 10 lakhs	4	6.8	14	3.2	28	
		> Rs..10 lakhs	0.8	1.2	1.2	0	3.2	
		Total	12.4	36.4	42.8	8.4	100	
6	Educational Qualification	SSC & below	1.2	6.0	2.4	1.2	10.8	.026
		Graduate	6.4	21.6	20.4	2.8	51.2	
		Post graduate & above	4.8	8.8	20.0	4.4	38.0	
		Total	12.4	36.4	42.8	8.4	100.0	

Source : Primary data

The above table reveals the following :

1. Age wise analysis reveals that. the customers in the age group of less than 25 years (5.2%) and above 50 years(24.4%) , majority of them i.e.42.8% are visiting the bank only once in a month. Whereas the customers in the age group of 25yrs to 50 yrs are visiting the bank once in a week.

2. Sex wise analysis reveals that on the whole there are no major deviations among male and female customers about visiting the bank. About 30% of the male and 13.2% of the female visit the bank only once in a month.

3. Computer skills, Occupation wise and Income wise analysis shows that there is no major differences about the frequency of visit to the bank within these groups.

4. Thus the above analysis reveals that cross tabulation analysis represents the same trend as in case of general trend as shown in table 4.5. It is found that most of the customers (42.8%) visit the banks once in a month followed by (36.4%) visiting once in a week.

5. Since the chi-square test value is less than .05, with respect to occupation and educational qualification of the respondents. We can conclude that there is no significant relationship between the frequency of visit to the bank and educational qualification and occupation of the respondents.

6. There is an association between the age, sex, annual income and computer skills of the respondents and the frequency of visit to the bank.

5.8 Time spent for bank transactions before and after BPR

One of the important purposes of BPR in the banks is to reduce the time taken for different kind of transactions while serving the customers. It is generally expected that BPR will result in speedy operations which in turn significantly reduce the time taken for completing the bank transactions. Here an attempt is made to understand the extent of time taken for different transactions before and after BPR. Their responses have been organised into three time ranges of three types as mentioned below :

Chart 5.1

Time range for various Banking Services

Time Range	Services
1. Less than 15 minutes 2. 15 to 30 minutes 3. More than 30 minutes	• Cash withdrawal • Withdrawal through cheques • Deposit of cash • Opening a new account • Obtaining demand draft or pay order • Updating the pass book
1. Less than 3 days 2. 3 to 5 days 3. More than 5 days	Clearance of local cheques
1. Less than 10 days 2. 10 to 20 days 3. More than 20 days	Clearance of outstation cheques

Average time taken for various transactions has been computed, before and after BPR and is presented in table no's: 5.6A to 5.6I

5.6A Time spent on withdrawal of cash before and after BPR

Customers keep their cash balances in the bank and withdraw as and when they need cash. We now examine the time spent by the customers in withdrawing cash before and after BPR Table no 5.6 discusses the time taken by the respondents for cash withdrawals at SBH before and after BPR.

Table 5.6A

Approximate time taken for Cash withdrawal

S.No.	Variables	Before BPR		After BPR	
		Frequency	Percent	Frequency	Percent
1	Less than 15 minutes	59	23.6	181	72.4
2	15 to 30 minutes	136	54.4	51	20.4
3	More than 30 minutes	55	22.0	18	7.2
Total		250	100.0	250	100.0
Average Time Taken		21min		13min	
Average Time Saved		8min			

Source : Primary data

Before BPR, customers were required to spare more time for withdrawal of cash and it is not so after BPR. It may be observed from the above table 4.6, that 72.4 % of the customers are able to withdraw cash from their accounts within 15 min after BPR, whereas it was only 23.6% of the respondents before BPR. Similarly, there has been a decline in the number of respondents waiting for more than30 minutes for withdrawal of cash after BPR. The average time taken reveals that before BPR it was 21min and after BPR it is 13min, average time saved due to BPR is found to be 8min. From these observations, it may be concluded that on account of BPR, customers are benefited in terms of time spent on withdrawal transactions.

5.6B Time taken for withdrawal through cheques before and after BPR

It is a known fact that there is a difference in withdrawal of cash and withdrawing through cheques. Further bank ensures the identification of the customer before the cheque is cleared for payment. This involves more time in making the payment to the customer

In this context an attempt has been made to ascertain the time spent by the customers for withdrawing cash through cheques. The relevant data is furnished in table 5.6B

Table 5.6B

Approximate time taken for Withdrawal through cheques

S.No.	Variables	Before BPR		After BPR	
		Frequency	Percent	Frequency	Percent
1	Less than 15 minutes	41	16.4	169	67.6
2	15 to 30 minutes	144	57.6	61	24.4
3	More than 30 minutes	65	26.0	20	8.0
Total		250	100.0	250	100.0
Average Time Taken		24min		14min	
Average Time Saved		10 min			

Source : Primary data

It may be noted from the above table that there has been a significant increase in the number of customers receiving cash within 15 minutes after BPR, 16.4% of the sample respondents expressed that they withdraw cash in 15 minutes, the rest were waiting for more than 15minutes. Further after BPR the number of customers drawing cash has gone up toy 67.6% of the total respondents. Further, it may be noted that only

24% of the customers were waiting for more than 15 minutes for withdrawing cash after BPR. The average time taken before BPR is 24minutes and after BPR is 14minutes, average time saved due to BPR is 10minutes.These observations again vindicate that BPR has benefited the customers. But we can make a note that more than30% of the respondents are spending more than 15 minutes, indicating some functional problems even after BPR.

5.6C Deposit of cash

Deposit of cash both in current account and savings accounts is one of the most commonly found banking transactions in the day to day operations of the bank. In some cases it may take 15 to 30 minutes and sometimes more than 30 minutes also. To verify the extent of BPR has helped the customers in the matter of deposit of cash. The relevant information was ascertained and is presented in table 5.6C.

Table 5.6C

Approximate time taken for Deposit of cash

S.No.	Variables	Before BPR		After BPR	
		Frequency	Percent	Frequency	Percent
1	Less than 15 minutes	55	22.0	166	66.4
2	15 to 30 minutes	149	59.6	55	22.0
3	More than 30 minutes	46	18.4	29	11.6
Total		250	100.0	250	100.0
Average Time Taken		22m		14m	
Average Time Saved		8m			

Source : Primary data

It may be noted from the above table that there has been a significant reduction in time spent by the customers for depositing cash after BPR. The table reveals the percentage of customers depositing cash within 15 minutes increased to 66.4% from 22% after BPR.

Similarly the percentage of customers waiting for 15 to 30 minutes declined from 59.6% to 22% after BPR. It may be noted that around 11.6% of the respondents are still waiting for more than 30 minutes indicating some technical problems.

The average time taken for depositing cash is 22 minutes before BPR and only 14minutes after BPR, average time saved in the process is 8 minutes, indicating an improvement in terms of time spent by the customers. Thus it is clear that the BPR benefited the customers in depositing cash.

5.6D Time taken for opening a new account in the bank before and after BPR

Generally whenever a customer wants to open an account with a bank he has to fulfil the formalities of opening the account such as filling the form, providing residential proof etc, thus requiring a good amount of time has to be spent at the bank. However, it is likely that implementation of BPR at SBH may reduce the time and thus improve the customer satisfaction. Table 5.9D furnishes the information in this regard.

Table 5.6D

Approximate time taken for opening a new account

S.No.	Variables	Before BPR		After BPR	
		Frequency	Percent	Frequency	Percent
1	Less than 15 minutes	22	8.8	126	50.4
2	15 to 30 minutes	111	44.4	58	23.2
3	More than 30 minutes	117	46.8	66	26.4
Total		250	100.0	250	100.0
Average Time Taken		28m		19m	
Average Time Saved		9m			

Source: Primary data

From the above table we can observe that 46.8% of the respondents have taken more than 30m minutes for opening a new account before BPR, whereas only 26.4% of the respondents are taking more than 30 minutes after BPR. Similarly customers taking less than 15 minutes for opening a new account, has increased from 8.8% of the respondents before BPR to 50.4 % after BPR. The average time taken for opening an account before BPR was 28 minutes whereas it is only 19 minutes after BPR, thus saving 9 minutes .The results of the survey clearly indicates that BPR has resulted in reduction of time but at the same time lot of improvement needs to be done in this regard as more than quarter i.e.26.4% of the respondents are taking more than 30 minutes for opening of the account.

5.6E Time taken for obtaining DD's and Pay orders

Issue of demand draft / pay orders to customers for varied purposes is another routine and major function of the bank. Information regarding the time spent on obtaining demand draft and pay orders before and after BPR is tabulated in the table below for analysis.

Table 5.6E

Approximate time taken for obtaining demand draft or pay order

S.No.	Variables	Before BPR		After BPR	
		Frequency	Percent	Frequency	Percent
1	Less than 15 minutes	27	10.8	124	49.6
2	15 to 30 minutes	131	52.4	74	29.6
3	More than 30 minutes	92	36.8	52	20.8
Total		250	100.0	250	100.0
Average Time Taken		26min		18min	
Average Time Saved		8 min			

Source : Primary data

It may be noted from the table 5.10, that there is a drastic improvement in the matter of issue of demand drafts and pay orders to customers after BPR .It is clear from the table that prior to BPR only 10.8% of the respondents were issued DD's in less than 15 minutes , whereas after BPR almost 50% of the respondents are receiving DD's and pay orders in less than 15 minutes .There is a slight decline in contrast to the number of respondents waiting for more than 30 minutes for similar transaction after BPR (i.e. from 36.8% to 20.8 %). The average time spent in availing the DD's and pay orders before BPR is 26 minutes and after BPR being 18 minutes, average time saved due to BPR is 8 minutes. These observations lead to a conclusion that there is a decline in the time spent by the customers on obtaining demand drafts and pay orders. As a result of BPR customer satisfaction has improved.

5.6F Time spent for updating the pass book

Customers frequently update their accounts to check/verify their balance and interests amounts, so as to check the balance calculated by the bank from time to time. Updating the pass book plays a crucial role in case of business and institutional customers, since this enables them to reconcile their accounts. Generally the updating of customer's bank account takes more time, if it is done manually. In this context BPR in banks has an important role to play. Table 4.11 provides the information pertaining to time spent by different customer's respondents on updating the pass book before and after BPR.

Table 5.6F

Approximate time taken for updating the pass book

S.No.	Variables	Before BPR		After BPR	
		Frequency	Percent	Frequency	Percent
1	Less than 15 minutes	45	18.0	165	66.0
2	15 to 30 minutes	149	59.6	57	22.8
3	More than 30 minutes	56	22.4	28	11.2
Total		250	100.0	250	100.0
Average Time Taken		23min		14min	
Average Time Saved		9 min			

Source : Primary data

It may be observes d from the table that there has been a remarkable improvement in the matter of time spent by the customers on this operation after BPR. Prior to BPR only 18% of the respondents were able to update their accounts within 15 minutes, whereas after BPR the percentage has gone up to 66%. At the same time from 22% of the respondents taking more than 30 minutes before BPR has reduced to half of it i.e. 11.2% after BPR. The average time spent by the respondents for updating /reconciling the pass book reveals that before BPR it was 23 minutes and after BPR is only 14 minutes, time saved due to BPR for updating the pass book is 9 minutes.

5.6G Time taken for Clearance of local cheques

One of the most important areas of the banking operations is clearance of cheques (both local and outstation cheques). Information pertaining to time spent by different respondents for clearance of local cheques is given in the following table 4.12.

Table 5.6G

Approximate time taken for Clearance of local cheques

S.No.	Variables	Before BPR		After BPR	
		Frequency	Percent	Frequency	Percent
1	Less than 3 days	36	14.4	156	62.4
2	3 to 5 days	145	58.0	67	26.8
3	More than 5 days	69	27.6	27	10.8
Total		250	100.0	250	100.0
Average Time Taken		4 days		3 days	
Average Time Saved		1 day			

Source : Primary data

It may be observed from the data provided in the table that there has been a remarkable improvement in the matter of time spent on clearance of local cheques after BPR in banks. Prior to BPR only 14.4% of the respondents were able to clear their local cheques in less than 3 days whereas after BPR this has gone up to 62.4%. The average time taken for clearance of local cheques before BPR is 4 days and after BPR is 3 days, average time saved is only 1 day for clearance of local cheques.

5.6H Time taken for Clearance of outstation cheques

One of the most frustrating transactions for the customers is clearance of out station cheques. In the Indian context, the time lag between deposit of the outstation cheque in an account and remittance of the amount into the account by bank is unduly high. Information pertaining to the time taken by the banks for clearance of outstation cheques is given in the following table 5.6H

Table 5.6H

Approximate time taken for Clearance of outstation cheques

S.No.	Variables	Before BPR		After BPR	
		Frequency	Percent	Frequency	Percent
1	Less than 10 days	59	23.6	169	67.6
2	10 to 20 days	127	50.8	50	20.0
3	More than 20 days	64	25.6	31	12.4
Total		250	100.0	250	100.0
Average Time Taken		15 days		9 days	
Average Time Saved		6 days			

Source : Primary data

From the above table we can observe that only 23.6% of the respondents only were taking less than 10 days for clearance of outstation cheques before BPR but after BPR 67.6% of the respondents are able to clear their outstation cheques within 10 days.12.4% of the sample respondents said that they are still taking more than 20 days to clear their outstation cheques. The average time taken to clear the outstation cheque before BPR is 15 days and after BPR is 9 days, thus time saved is 6 days i.e. almost one week. Hence the survey clearly indicates that a lot of improvement needs to be made towards reducing the time taken for clearance of out station cheques.

The average time taken for the various banking transactions before and after BPR are presented in table 5.6I below -

Table No. 5.6 I

Average time taken for banking transactions before and after BPR - Customers Protection

S.No.	Transaction	Before BPR	After BPR	Time Saved
1	Cash withdrawal	21min	13min	8min
2	Withdrawal through cheques	24min	14min	10min
3	Deposit of cash	22m	14m	8min
4	Time spent in opening a new account	28m	19m	9min
5	Obtaining demand draft or pay order	26min	18min	8min
6	Time spent on updating the pass book	23min	14min	9min
7	Clearance of local cheques	4days	3days	1day
8	Clearance of outstation cheques	15days	9days	6days

Source : Primary data

Thus we can conclude that BPR has resulted in saving time of the customers with respect to all the services rendered by the bank.

5.9 Level of satisfaction for BPR in banking services at SBH

The prime objective of BPR in banks is to enhance the customer satisfaction and serve the customers effectively. It is expected that customer's satisfaction level increases with BPR, since it results in undergoing rapid and radical changes driven by technology, innovation in products and services and ever expanding customer expectations.

With a view to examine the level of satisfaction among customers after BPR at SBH, the respondents were asked to indicate their satisfaction for select services on a five point liker's scale with the responses. 1) Highly satisfied, 2) Satisfied, 3) Neither satisfied nor dissatisfied, 4) Dissatisfied and 5) Highly dissatisfied. The responses are tabulated and shown in the table no 4.14 for the purpose of analyses.

Table 5.7

Level of Satisfaction

S.No.	Particulars	Rank 1	Rank 2	Rank 3	Rank 4	Rank 5
1	Multi – Service on a single counter	38	142	34	21	15
	% of respondents	15	**57**	14	8	6
2	ATM/ Debit Card Service	81	133	19	15	2
	% of respondents	32	**53**	8	6	1
3	Credit Card Service	29	139	38	6	5
	% of respondents	13	**64**	18	3	2
4	Anywhere Banking	32	137	31	4	-
	% of respondents	17	**74**	17	2	-
5	Internet Banking	32	102	38	4	8
	% of respondents	17	**55**	21	2	4
6	Fund Transfer	26	84	50	7	3
	% of respondents	15	**49**	29	4	2
7	E- Cheque	17	63	52	14	7
	% of respondents	11	**41**	34	9	5

Source : Primary data

It is found from the above table majority of the respondents have indicated "satisfied" for all the services, like 57%of the respondents are satisfied with multi- service on single counter, 53% are satisfied with ATM/Debit card, 64% with credit card services, 74% if the customers with anywhere banking, 55% of them with internet banking, 49% for fund transfer and 41% with E-cheque facilities. This indicates that the respondents are satisfied with the same but much more needs to be done in banks. Less than 20% of the respondents are" highly satisfied" with the services.

Efforts are being made to quantify the level of satisfaction of the customers by allotting scores, and calculating the average score as follows.

The following Scores have been assigned for their responses.

Scale	Scores
Highly satisfied	5
Satisfied	4
Neither satisfies nor dissatisfied	3
Dissatisfied	2
Highly dissatisfied	1

Weighted scores have been computed by multiplying the number of responses with the respective scores. Sum of these weighted scores are calculated for each type of service provided by banks. Weighted average scores have been computed and shown in the following table 5.8

Table 5.8

Level of satisfaction of customers on BPR initiatives

S.No.	Services	Weighted scores	Average scores
1	Multi – Service on a single counter	917	3.67
2	ATM/ Debit Card Service	1026	4.10
3	Credit Card Service	832	3.33
4	Anywhere Banking	809	3.24
5	Internet Banking	698	2.79
6	Fund Transfer	633	2.53
7	E- Cheque	498	1.99
Total weighted Score		**5413**	
Weighted Average		**3.09**	

Source : Primary data

It may be observed from the table that weighted averages of all the services except E-cheque are above 2.5, which means that customer's satisfaction is above average. Average of combined scores also represents fairly high level of satisfaction (3.09). Highest satisfaction is noticed in case of ATM/Debit card services followed by Multi-Service on a single counter, Credit card service, anywhere banking and other services.

5.10 Customer's level of satisfaction vs. demographic variables :

After identifying the customer satisfaction level of BPR in banks as perceived by sample customers, an attempt is made to find out whether there is any difference in analysis based on the demographic variables such as age, sex, income, educational qualifications, and occupation of the respondents and the customers' level of satisfaction. For this purpose cross tabulation of variables are made and presented in the following tables.

5.9A Age vs. Satisfaction of the customers :

The table below explains the satisfaction of customers with respect to various services according to different age groups.

Table 5.9A

Age VS. Satisfaction of the customers

S.No.	Particulars	< 25 years		25 to 50 years		> 50 years	
		WS	AS	WS	AS	WS	AS
1	Multi–Service on a single counter	102	3.92	415	3.99	414	3.45
2	ATM/Debit Card Service	102	3.88	440	4.23	463	3.86
3	Credit Card Service	73	2.81	365	3.51	390	3.25
4	Anywhere Banking	87	3.35	359	3.45	406	3.38
5	Internet Banking	55	2.12	445	4.47	351	2.93
6	Fund Transfer	58	2.22	299	2.88	331	2.76
7	E- Cheque	43	1.65	258	2.48	297	2.48

Source: Primary data

Age wise analysis in table no 4.16 shows that highest satisfaction in case of below 25 years is found in Multi-service single counter and ATM/Debit card service, in the age group of 25 to 50 years, it is internet banking having the highest score of 4.47 followed by ATM/Debit card service, and in the third category i.e. above 50 years, respondents have the maximum satisfaction with ATM/Debit card services (3.86) and 3.45 for Multi – service on a single counter.

Further to study whether the age of the respondents are independent of the level of satisfaction of the various BPR initiatives, chi-square test was calculated. It was found that there is no significant relationship between age and the various services such as Multi – Service on a single counter, ATM/ Debit Card Service, anywhere banking, internet banking, fund transfer and e-cheque (0.011,0. 006,0.002,0.000,0.002,0.038). Whereas, the study indicates that there is a significant relationship between age of the respondents and credit card services (.212).

5.9B Gender vs. Satisfaction of the customers :

Having seen the relationship of age of the respondents and the satisfaction level of the customers, efforts are made to study the relationship between gender of the respondent and the various reengineered services provided by the bank in the table below.

Table 5.9B

Gender vs. Satisfaction of the customers

S.No.	Particulars	Male		Female	
		W.S	A.S	W.S	A.S
1	Multi – Service on a single counter	664	3.65	263	3.87
2	ATM/ Debit Card Service	724	3.98	276	4.06
3	Credit Card Service	601	3.30	233	3.43
4	Anywhere Banking	634	3.48	214	3.15
5	Internet Banking	490	2.69	193	2.84
6	Fund Transfer	633	3.48	246	3.57
7	E- Cheque	443	2.43	171	2.51

Source : Primary data

From the above table it is clear that gender wise analysis reveals that relatively high level of satisfaction among female respondents with 4.06 as compared to the male customers with 3.98 is found for ATM/Debit card services followed by multi –service on Single counter. Female respondents rated credit card services as third whereas male respondents are satisfied with anywhere banking. Least score is for internet banking for both male and female customers.

The study reveals that there is no significant relationship between gender of the respondents and the multi service on single counter (chi square test p-value is .005). It was also found that there is a significant relationship between gender and the various services such as ATM/Debit Card Service, credit card services, anywhere banking, internet banking, fund transfer and e-cheque (.928, .944, .388, 315, .315, .402).

5.9C Educational Qualification vs. Satisfaction of the customers :

The table below indicates the relationship between the educational qualification of the respondents and the satisfaction of the customers.

Table 5.9C

Educational Qualification vs. Satisfaction of the customers

S.No.	Particulars	SSC & Below		Graduation		Post Graduate & Above	
		WS	AS	WS	AS	WS	AS
1	Multi – Service on a single counter	103	3.68	481	3.76	347	3.69
2	ATM/ Debit Card Service	128	4.57	530	4.14	378	4.02
3	Credit Card Service	106	3.79	445	3.46	287	3.05
4	Anywhere Banking	118	3.86	459	3.59	297	3.16
5	Internet Banking	102	3.64	464	3.63	335	3.56
6	Fund Transfer	88	3.14	456	3.56	322	3.43
7	E- Cheque	92	3.29	422	3.30	302	3.21

Source : Primary data

Education wise analysis shows that irrespective of their qualification all the three groups have the highest level of satisfaction with respect to ATM/Debit card services. The respondents of 1st group (SSC and below) have rated anywhere banking as second, credit card service as third followed by multi - service in single counter. Graduates and post graduates have rated multi - service in single counter as second and third as internet banking services. Graduates preferred fund transfer as fourth, where as post graduates rated anywhere banking as fourth.

To study whether the education qualification of the respondents are independent of the level of satisfaction of the various BPR initiatives, chi-square test was calculated. And it was found that there is no significant relationship between educational qualification of the respondent and the various services such as, ATM/ Debit Card Service, credit card services, anywhere banking, fund transfer (.018, .000, .009, and .001). Whereas, the study further indicates that there is a significant relationship between educational qualification of the respondents and services such as Multi – Service on a single counter, internet banking, and e-cheque (.396, .818, and .204).

5.9D Income Vs Satisfaction of the customers :

The table below explains the satisfaction of customers with respect to various services according to the annual income of the respondents.

Table 5.9D

Income Vs Satisfaction of the customers

S.No.	Particulars	Below Rs. 5 Lakhs		Rs. 5 Lakhs to Rs. 10 Lakhs		Above Rs. 10 Lakhs	
		WS	AS	WS	AS	WS	AS
1	Multi – Service on a single counter	632	3.67	266	3.80	33	4.13
2	ATM/ Debit Card Service	707	4.11	258	3.69	36	4.5
3	Credit Card Service	561	3.26	221	3.16	27	3.38
4	Anywhere Banking	665	3.87	265	3.79	35	4.38
5	Internet Banking	604	3.51	267	3.81	30	3.75
6	Fund Transfer	595	3.46	256	3.64	23	2.88
7	E- Cheque	365	2.12	299	4.27	24	4.0

Source : Primary data

From the above table it is evident that the respondents having income of less than Rs.5 lakhs, have highest level of satisfaction with respect to ATM/Debit card service followed by anywhere banking , multi – service on a single counter and internet banking. Customers with the annual income of Rs.5 lakhs and 10 lakhs have highest satisfaction with internet banking, followed by multi – service on single counter, anywhere banking and ATM/Debit card services. Respondents with an annual income of more than Rs. 5 lakhs have highest satisfaction with ATM/Debit card service followed by anywhere banking, multi – service on single counter and internet banking.

The study reveals that there is no significant relationship between annual income of the respondents and the fund transfer and e-cheque services (chi square test p- value is .000, .003). It was also found that there is a significant relationship between annual income of the respondents and the various services such as multi service on single counter, ATM/ Debit Card Service, credit card services, anywhere banking, and internet banking, (.157, .348, .280, .284, and .327).

5.9E Type of Account vs. Satisfaction of the customers :

The table below indicates the relationship between the type of account of the respondents and the satisfaction of the customers.

Table 5.9E

Type of Account vs. Satisfaction of the customers

S.No.	Particulars	Savings a/c		Current a/c	
		W.S	A.S	W.S	A.S
1	Multi – Service on a single counter	854	3.80	77	3.08
2	ATM/ Debit Card Service	939	4.17	96	3.84
3	Credit Card Service	840	3.73	91	3.64
4	Anywhere Banking	866	3.85	99	3.96
5	Internet Banking	829	3.68	82	2.67
6	Fund Transfer	789	3.51	90	3.60
7	E- Cheque	624	2.77	111	4.44

Source : Primary data

From the above table it is clear that the respondents having saving bank account in the banks have highest satisfaction with ATM/Debit card service, followed by anywhere banking, multi – service on single counter and credit card service respectively .Current account holders have highest satisfaction with anywhere banking, followed by ATM/Debit card service, credit card service and fund transfer respectively.

Further to study whether the nature of account of the respondents are independent of the level of satisfaction of the various BPR initiatives, chi-square tests were calculated. It was found that there is no significant relationship between nature of account and the various services such as Multi – Service on a single counter, credit card services, internet banking, and fund transfer (.003, .014, .000, .058). Whereas, the study indicates that there is a significant relationship between the nature of account of the respondents and satisfaction of the customers with respect to services such as ATM/ Debit Card Service, anywhere banking, and e-cheque (.504, .519, and .560).

5.9F Computer skills Vs. Satisfaction of the customers :

The table below indicates the relationship between the knowledge of the computer skills of the respondents and the satisfaction of the customers.

Table 5.9F

Computer skills Vs. Satisfaction of the customers

S.No.	Particulars	Yes		No	
		W.S	A.S	W.S	A.S
1	Multi – Service on a single counter	498	3.69	433	3.77
2	ATM/ Debit Card Service	562	4.16	471	4.10
3	Credit Card Service	524	3.86	406	3.53
4	Anywhere Banking	518	3.84	434	3.77
5	Internet Banking	483	3.58	318	2.77
6	Fund Transfer	474	3.51	400	3.48
7	E- Cheque	435	3.22	399	3.47

Source : Primary data

According to knowledge of computer skills of the respondents, it is interesting to note that respondents irrespective of computer knowledge have highest satisfaction with ATM/Debit card service. Respondents with computer knowledge have rated anywhere banking, credit card service and multi – service on single counter as second, third and fourth respectively. Customers having no computer knowledge have rated anywhere banking and multi – service on single counter as second, followed by credit card service etc.

The study reveals that there is no significant relationship between the knowledge of computer skills of the respondents and the services such as fund transfer and e-cheque services (chi square test p- value is .001, .012). It was also found that there is a significant relationship between knowledge of computer skills of the respondents and the various services such as multi service on single counter, ATM/ Debit Card Service, credit card services, anywhere banking, and internet banking, (.743, .312, .144, .069, and .078).

5.11 Customers perception about impact of BPR

To study the impact of BPR in banks on customers, employees and bank performance, an attempt is made to study the same from the point of view of selected bank customers and their responses have been arranged on a five point rating scale ranging from 1) High Impact, 2) Moderate, 3) Little Impact, 4) No Impact and 5) Adverse impact. For this purpose an appropriate weights have been given for the responses as shown below.

Scale	High Impact	Moderate	Little Impact	No Impact	Adverse impact
Scores	5	4	3	2	1

Weighted scores and averages have been computed by multiplying with the number of respondents and with the weights concerned weights. Sum of these weighted scores are calculated for each variable to know the impact of BPR on customers, on employees and on bank performance. Weighted average scores and averages have been computed and shown in the following table 5.10

Table 5.10

Impact of BPR

S.No.	Particulars	Weighted Score	Average Score
1	On Customers	1013	4.05
2	On Employees	978	3.91
3	On Bank Performance	981	3.92
Total weighted Score		2972	
Weighted Average		3.96	

Source : Primary data

It is evident from the above table that the sample customers feel that the impact of BPR is much "on customers" (4.05) followed by "Banks performance" (3.92) and "on employees" (3.91) .On the whole we can conclude that customers are more satisfied due to BPR in banks.

5.12 Demographic variables of the respondents and the customers perception on BPR and its impact on customer satisfaction, employees and bank performance:

After identifying the impact of BPR in banks on customers, on employees and on bank performance as perceived by sample customers an attempt is made to further probe whether there are any differences in perceptions according to demographic variables like age, sex, income etc. Analysis is made for each of these variables and weighted score and average scores were computed for quality analysis and presented in the following tables.

5.11A Age vs. Impact of BPR :

The study makes an attempt to analyse the relationship (if any), between the age of respondents and impact of BPR.

Table No. 5.11A

Age vs. Impact of BPR

Age	Impact on Customers		Impact on employees		Impact on bank performance	
	W.S	A.S	W.S	A.S	W.S	A.S
< 25 yrs	109	4.19	102	3.9	107	4.12
25-50 yrs	425	4.09	409	3.93	420	4.04
Above 50 yrs	473	3.94	475	3.96	446	3.72

Source : Primary data

Age wise analysis shows that respondents of less than 25 years have highest average score of 4.19 for impact of BPR on customers, whereas the impact on employees have a highest score of 3.93 against the respondents in the age group of 25 to 50 years and once again the respondents with less than 25 years have the maximum average score of 4.12 on impact of BPR on bank performance.

The chi-square test values are .020, .000, .026, thus we can conclude that there is no significant relationship between the age of the respondents and the impact of BPR.

5.11B Gender vs. Impact of BPR :

Having studied the relationship of age of the respondents and the impact of BPR, efforts are made to study the relationship between gender of the respondents and the impact of BPR, are analysed and presented in the table below :

Table No. 5.11B

Gender vs. Impact of BPR

Gender	Impact on Customers		Impact on employees		Impact on bank performance	
	W.S	A.S	W.S	A.S	W.S	A.S
Male	733	4.03	727	3.99	716	3.93
Female	270	3.97	259	3.81	253	3.72

Source : Primary data

It is evident from gender wise analysis that the male counter parts are able to respondent positively with the highest average score of 4.03, 3.99 and 3.93 for the impact of BPR on customers, employees and bank performance respectively.

The study further confirms that there is a significant relationship of the gender of the respondents and the impact of BPR (0.755, 0.268, and 0.352)

5.11C Educational Qualification vs. Impact of BPR :

It is further studied to analyse the relationship (if any), between the educational qualification of respondents and impact of BPR. The analysis is presented in the table below :

Table No. 5.11C

Educational Qualification vs. Impact of BPR

Educational Qualification	Impact on Customers		Impact on employees		Impact on bank performance	
	W.S	A.S	W.S	A.S	W.S	A.S
SSC and below	114	4.07	109	3.89	105	3.75
Graduate	524	4.09	512	4.0	499	3.9
Post graduate and above	368	3.91	361	3.84	365	3.88

Source : Primary data

According to educational qualification wise analysis shows that the graduate respondents have the maximum average score of 4.09, 4.0 and 3.90 respectively for impact on customers, employees and bank performance.

From the chi-square tests values (0.385, 0.001, 0.000), we can conclude that there is significant relationship between the educational qualification of the respondents and the impact of BPR on customers. At the same we find that there is no significant relationship between the educational qualification of the respondents and the impact of BPR on employees and on bank performance.

5.11D Computer Skills vs. Impact of BPR :

The impact of BPR with respect to the knowledge of computer skills of the respondents are presented in the table below :

Table No. 5.11D

Computer Skills vs. Impact of BPR

Computer skills	Impact on Customers		Impact on employees		Impact on bank performance	
	W.S	A.S	W.S	A.S	W.S	A.S
Yes	538	3.99	526	3.90	521	3.86
No	469	4.08	450	3.91	452	3.93

Source : Primary data

It is interesting to note from the table, that according to computer knowledge of the respondents, it is the respondents having no computer knowledge have rated high with the maximum average score of 4.08, 3.91 and 3.93 for the impact of BPR in banks on customers, employees and on bank performance respectively.

We can further conclude that there is significant relationship between the knowledge of computer skills of the respondents and the impact of BPR on customers and on bank performance (0.450 and 0.091). At the same we find that there is no significant relationship between the knowledge of computer skills of the respondents and the impact of BPR on employees (0.030).

5.11EOccupation vs. Impact of BPR :

The study tries to analyse the relationship (if any), between the occupation of respondents and impact of BPR. The analysis is presented in the table below –

Table No. 5.11E

Occupation vs. Impact of BPR

Occupation	Impact on Customers		Impact on employees		Impact on bank performance	
	W.S	A.S	W.S	A.S	W.S	A.S
Business	137	4.15	141	4.27	127	3.85
Employment	559	3.88	569	3.95	574	3.99
Others	295	4.04	276	3.78	272	3.73

Source : Primary data

Occupation wise analysis, it is the respondents doing business have the maximum average score of 4.15, 4.27 and 3.85 for the impact of BPR on customers, employees and bank performance respectively.

We can conclude that there is significant relationship between the occupation of the respondents and the impact of BPR on customers (chi-square p value is 0.316). At the same we find that there is no significant relationship between the occupation of the respondents and the impact of BPR on employees and on bank performance (chi-square p value is 0.000 & 0.012).

5.11F Income vs. Impact of BPR :

The impact of BPR with respect to the annual Income of the respondents are presented in the table below :

Table No. 5.11F

Income vs. Impact of BPR

Income	Impact on Customers		Impact on employees		Impact on bank performance	
	W.S	A.S	W.S	A.S	W.S	A.S
Less than Rs. 5 lakhs	689	4.01	672	3.91	672	3.91
Rs. 5 lakhs - Rs10 lakhs	282	4.03	276	3.94	301	4.30
Above Rs. 10 lakhs	36	4.5	38	4.75	38	4.75

Source : Primary data

As regards to income wise analysis it is the respondents having an annual income of more than Rs. 10 lakhs have the highest score of 4.5, 4.75 and 4.75 for the impact of BPR in banks on customers, employees and on bank performance respectively.

We can conclude that there is no significant relationship between the annual income of the respondents and the impact of BPR on customers. At the same we find that there is a significant relationship between the annual income of the respondents and the impact of BPR on employees and on bank performance (0.018, 0.088, and 0.264).

5.11G Nature of account vs. Impact of BPR :

The study tries to analyse the relationship (if any), between the nature of account of respondents and impact of BPR. The analysis is presented in the table below :

Table No. 5.11G

Nature of Account vs. Impact of BPR

Nature of account	Impact on Customers		Impact on employees		Impact on bank performance	
	W.S	A.S	W.S	A.S	W.S	A.S
Savings account	912	4.05	882	3.92	891	3.96
Current account	95	3.80	104	4.16	82	3.28

Source : Primary data

According to the type of account, respondents with savings bank account have the highest average score of 4.05 and 3.96 for the impact of BPR on customers and bank performance respectively. Respondents with current account in the bank have the maximum score of 4.16 for the impact of BPR on employees of the bank.

From the chi-square tests values (0.364, 0.511, 0.001), we can conclude that there is significant relationship between the nature of account of the respondents and the impact of BPR on customers and on employees. At the same we find that there is no significant relationship between the nature of account of the respondents and the impact of BPR on bank performance.

5.13 Customers level of awareness and Usage of banking services :

The benefits of BPR in banks can reach the customers, if they are aware of these services. Further the rate of usage of services among the customers who are aware of the services also indicates the effectiveness of BPR in banks. Therefore an attempt is made here to know about the number of customers who are aware of the services of banks and also the extent of usage of services. The percentage figures of customers who are aware and those who use these services are presented in the table 5.12.

Table No. 5.12

Customers level of awareness and Usage of banking services (%)

S.No.	Banking Services	Awareness	Usage	% of usage among awareness
1	Cash withdrawals	100	82.4	82.4
2	Cash Deposits	100	84	84
3	Demand Drafts/ Pay Orders	94	80.4	86
4	Cheque Deposits	86.8	74.8	86
5	ATM/Debit Card facilities	92.8	76	82
6	Credit Card Facilities	77.6	44.8	58
7	Grahak Mitras	35.2	14	40
8	Drop Boxes	76.8	48	63
9	Locker Facilities	76.4	42.8	56
10	Loans	79.2	44.8	57
11	Internet Banking	62.8	18.4	29
12	Anywhere Banking	55.6	28	50
13	Fund transfer	50	18.8	38
14	Foreign Exchange	40	14	35
TOTAL		1027.2	671.2	846.4
Average of awareness and usage		73.37	47.94	60.46

Source : Primary data

1. It may be observed from the table that average percentage of awareness of banking services is high (73.37%), but the percentage of customers using these services is relatively low (47.94%).About 60.46% of respondents who are aware are using these services. Highest level of awareness is found in case of cash withdrawals, cash deposits, Demand drafts and pay orders etc.

2. It is interesting to note that Grahak Mitras a front office initiative for guiding the customers in conducting their transactions smoothly and helping them in choosing alternate delivery channels like ATM cards, internet banking, etc. , is having the lowest percentage of awareness among respondents.

3. To expedite and facilitate easier Cheque tendering, the Bank has provided specially designed drop boxes at 204 centres covering 473 branches. From the above table it is encouraging to note that 78.6% of the respondents are aware of this facility and 63% of them are using the same.

5.13 Benefits of BPR in Banks

BPR plays a vital role in banks since it offers many benefits to customers. For this purpose, twelve benefits have been identified based on discussions with customers and review of literature and customers are asked to identify and also rank the benefits in order of their preferences. The results thus obtained are tabulated and presented in the table below -

Table 5.13

Benefits of BPR to customers

S.No.	Particulars	R1	R2	R3	R4	R5	R6	R7	R8	R9	R10	R11	R12
1	Time Saving	170	40	3	4	27	-	2	2	2	-	-	-
		68	16	1.2	1.6	10.8	-	.8	.8	.8	-	-	-
2	Fastness in Services	23	131	31	26	4	12	2	-	2	16	3	-
		9.2	52.4	12.4	10.4	1.6	4.8	.8	-	.8	6.4	1.2	-
3	Home Banking Facilities	7	2	39	65	12	22	4	3	32	16	27	21
		2.8	.8	15.6	26	4.8	8.8	1.6	1.2	12.8	6.4	10.4	8.4
4	Easy payments of dues through bank	-	7	89	48	16	19	28	22	6	10	-	5
		-	2.8	35.6	19.2	6.4	7.6	11.2	8.8	2.4	4	-	2
5	Transparency in facilities	-	6	28	32	52	33	18	20	27	12	17	5
		-	2.4	11.2	12.8	20.8	13.2	7.2	8	10.8	4.8	6.8	2

6	Better transfer of funds	4	-	13	12	54	52	29	23	14	27	6	16
		1.6	-	5.2	4.8	21.6	20.8	11.6	9.2	5.6	10.8	2.4	6.4
7	Easy Clearances	-	11	10	17	9	57	67	40	29	-	10	-
		-	4.4	4	6.8	3.6	22.8	26.8	16	11.6	-	4	-
8	Easy balance enquiry	8	25	4	10	44	11	22	95	18	5	6	-
		3.2	10	1.6	4	17.6	4.4	8.8	38	7.2	2	2.4	-
9	Round the clock services	16	10	17	14	18	2	27	10	85	17	10	24
		6.4	4	6.8	5.6	7.2	.8	10.8	4	34	6.8	4	9.6
10	Minimizing chances of fraud	4	8	6	6	-	4	27	25	2	81	30	57
		1.6	3.2	2.4	2.4		1.6	10.8	10	.8	32.4	12	22.8
11	Hassle free in handling of cash	6	2	2	15	8	17	14	8	32	31	108	4
		2.4	.8	.8	6	3.2	6.8	5.6	3.2	12.8	12.4	43.2	1.6
12	Improved customer services	15	8	12	2	4	18	12	2	3	35	24	109
		6	3.2	4.8	.8	1.6	7.2	4.8	.8	1.2	14	9.6	43.6

Source : Primary data

From the above table, it is evident that 68% of the respondents ranked time saving as the top most benefit of BPR and ranked the same as first.52.4% of the respondent considered fastness of services as second most benefit of BPR.43.6% of the respondents felt that BPR has resulted in improved customer services, 43.2% of the respondents said that hassle free handling of cash as the other advantage of BPR maybe because of their awareness and usage of the alternate delivery channels such as ATM/Debit card facilities, anywhere banking internet banking etc. The other benefits as per their order of priority are easy payment of dues through bank, easy balance enquiry, round the clock services etc.

Efforts were made to quantify their ranks by giving score of 12 to 1.as shown in the table given :

Ranks	1	2	3	4	5	6	7	8	9	10	11	12
Weights	12	11	10	9	8	7	6	5	4	3	2	1

Weighted scores have been computed for each of the identified benefit and ranks are assigned according to the scores obtained. These results are shown in table no 5.14.

Table 5.14

Customer's perceptions on benefits of BPR in banks

S.No.	Particulars	Score	Ranks
1	Time Saving	2784	1
2	Fastness in Services	2453	2
3	Home Banking Facilities	1621	6
4	Easy payments of dues through bank	1987	4
5	Transparency in facilities	1464	9
6	Better transfer of funds	1521	7
7	Easy Clearances	1473	8
8	Easy balance enquiry	1636	5
9	Round the clock services	2077	3
10	Minimizing chances of fraud	903	12
11	Hassle free in handling of cash	997	10
12	Improved customer services	920	11

Source : Primary data

It may be observed from the above table that majority of respondents felt that "Time Savings" is top most benefit, followed by "fastness in service"," round the clock service", easy payments of dues through bank, easy balance enquiry, home banking facilities and so on.

5.15 Relationship of demographic variables of the respondents and customers perceptions on benefits of BPR services

Demographic variables such as age, sex, educational qualification, computer skills, income, and type of account of the respondents and their relationship with the customers perceptions on benefits of BPR are being analysed and presented in tables 5.15A to 5.15G.

5.15A Age vs. Customers perceptions on benefits of BPR services :

Customers perceptions on benefits of BPR services according to the age of the respondents are presented below :

Table 5.15A

Age vs. Customers perceptions on benefits of BPR services

S.No.	Particulars	< 25 years		25 to 50 years		> 50 years	
		AS	Rank	Rank	AS	AS	Rank
1	Time Saving	8.85	1	10.56	1	10.07	1
2	Fastness in Services	7.62	3	8.23	2	8.89	2
3	Home Banking Facilities	3.93	8	4.24	8	5.27	6
4	Easy payments of dues through bank	8.08	2	5.82	4	8.07	3
5	Transparency in facilities	5.08	5	4.79	6	4.93	7
6	Better transfer of funds	3.89	9	3.92	9	4.43	9
7	Easy Clearances	5.92	4	4.28	7	4.88	8
8	Easy balance enquiry	4.3	7	7.44	3	5.74	4
9	Round the clock services	4.42	6	5.40	5	6.05	5
10	Minimizing chances of fraud	2.77	10	3.21	11.5	3.25	12
11	Hassle free in handling of cash	2.44	11	3.21	11.5	3.40	10
12	Improved customer services	2.31	12	3.37	10	3.39	11

Source : Primary data

Irrespective of age, all the respondents have ranked time saving as the foremost benefit of BPR. Respondents of below 25years of age considered easy payment of dues through banks, fastness in services, easy clearance, transparency in facilities as few other benefits of BPR in their order of priority. The respondents above 25 years , in the age group of 25 to 50 years and above 50 years have rated almost similarly the following as the major benefits of BPR as perceived by them namely – fastness in services, easy balance enquiry, easy payments of dues through banks and round the clock services.

5.15B Gender vs. Customers perceptions on benefits of BPR services :

Gender wise analysis is made with respect to the benefits of BPR and presented in the table below :

Table 5.15B

Gender vs. Customers perceptions on benefits of BPR services

S.No.	Particulars	MALE		FEMALE	
		AS	Rank	AS	Rank
1	Time Saving	10.12	1	10.28	1
2	Fastness in Services	8.82	2	7.26	2
3	Home Banking Facilities	4.86	7	4.26	7
4	Easy payments of dues through bank	5.57	4	5.26	5
5	Transparency in facilities	5.16	6	4.16	8
6	Better transfer of funds	4.31	9	3.76	9
7	Easy Clearances	4.71	8	4.79	6
8	Easy balance enquiry	6.17	3	6.91	3
9	Round the clock services	5.29	5	6.49	4
10	Minimizing chances of fraud	2.64	12	3.29	10
11	Hassle free in handling of cash	3.22	11	3.22	12
12	Improved customer services	3.34	10	3.24	11

Source : Primary data

Both male and female respondents have rated time saving, easy balance enquiry as the topmost benefits derived through BPR in banks. Male respondents have ranked easy payments of dues through banks and round the clock services as 4th and 5th, whereas a reverse ranking is noted among the female respondents.

5.15C Educational qualification vs. Customers perceptions on benefits of BPR services :

Customers perceptions on benefits of BPR services is analysed and presented according to the educational qualification of the respondents in the table below -

Table 5.15C

Educational qualification vs. Customers perceptions on benefits of BPR services

S.No.	Particulars	SSC and below		Graduation		Post graduation	
		AS	Rank	AS	Rank	AS	Rank
1	Time Saving	10.10	1	10.24	1	9.85	1
2	Fastness in Services	8.52	3	8.23	2	8.01	2
3	Home Banking Facilities	5.74	6	4.26	7	5.00	7
4	Easy payments of dues through bank	5.70	7	5.16	5	5.96	4
5	Transparency in facilities	5.85	5	4.25	8	5.23	5
6	Better transfer of funds	4.85	10	3.71	9	4.59	9
7	Easy Clearances	5.56	8	4.44	6	4.90	8
8	Easy balance enquiry	6.59	4	6.11	3	6.56	3
9	Round the clock services	8.59	2	5.39	4	5.06	6
10	Minimizing chances of fraud	3.63	12	2.09	12	3.68	11
11	Hassle free in handling of cash	5.22	9	2.84	10	3.51	12
12	Improved customer services	3.74	11	2.57	11	4.19	10

Source: Primary data

From the above table it is evident that all the respondents irrespective of their educational qualification considered time saving as the primary benefit of BPR to the customers. Respondents having SSC and below as their qualification have ranked rounds the clock services as second and fastness in services as3rd. Both graduates and post graduates had a similar view as they ranked second to fastness in services as second and round the clock services as third.

5.15D Knowledge in computer skills vs. Customers perceptions on benefits of BPR services :

Customers perceptions based on the knowledge of computer skills of the respondents is analysed and presented in the table below -

Table 5.15D

Knowledge in computer skills vs. Customers perceptions on benefits of BPR services

S.No.	Particulars	Yes		No	
		AS	Rank	AS	Rank
1	Time Saving	10.37	1	10.28	1
2	Fastness in Services	7.91	2	8.97	2
3	Home Banking Facilities	3.93	8	5.60	4
4	Easy payments of dues through bank	4.82	5	5.54	6
5	Transparency in facilities	4.37	6	5.49	8
6	Better transfer of funds	3.25	10	5.22	9
7	Easy Clearances	4.18	7	5.53	7
8	Easy balance enquiry	7.22	3	6.06	3
9	Round the clock services	5.44	4	5.81	5
10	Minimizing chances of fraud	2.40	12	3.41	11
11	Hassle free in handling of cash	2.71	11	3.81	10
12	Improved customer services	3.28	9	3.34	12

Source : Primary data

From the above table we find that all the respondents (irrespective of whether they have computer skills or not) considered time saving, fastness in services and easy balance enquiry as the major benefits of BPR in banks to customers. Respondents with computer skills have rated round the clock services as fourth, followed by easy payments of dues through banks as fifth. Whereas the respondents without computer skills considered home banking facilities as fourth and round the clock services as fifth.

5.15E Occupation vs. Customers perceptions on benefits of BPR services :

Customers perceptions based on the occupation of the respondents is analysed and presented in the table below :

Table 5.15E

Occupation vs. Customers perceptions on benefits of BPR services

S.No.	Particulars	Business		Employment		Others	
		AS	Rank	AS	Rank	AS	Rank
1	Time Saving	9.97	1	10.48	1	11.38	1
2	Fastness in Services	8.94	2	8.03	2	8.89	2
3	Home Banking Facilities	7.18	3	3.38	8	6.16	7
4	Easy payments of dues through bank	6.42	6	4.25	5	7.45	3
5	Transparency in facilities	6.85	4	2.79	10	5.84	8
6	Better transfer of funds	3.70	9	3.62	7	5.48	9
7	Easy Clearances	5.55	7	3.80	6	6.27	5
8	Easy balance enquiry	5.36	8	6.67	3	6.22	6
9	Round the clock services	6.45	5	5.02	4	6.40	4
10	Minimizing chances of fraud	2.58	12	1.99	12	4.78	11
11	Hassle free in handling of cash	2.76	11	2.51	11	4.82	10
12	Improved customer services	3.15	10	2.99	9	4.01	12

Source : Primary data

From the above table all the respondents have felt that time saving and fatness in services as the major benefits of BPR in banks. Respondents doing business considered home loan facilities, transparency in facilities and the round the clock services as few other major benefits of BPR in banks to customers in order of their priority. Employed respondents rated easy balance enquiry, round the clock services and easy payment of dues through banks, as few of the benefits of BPR, other respondents most of them being students felt easy payment of dues through banks round the clock services and easy balance enquiry as other benefits in order of their priority.

5.15F The type of account vs. Customers perceptions on benefits of BPR services :

Analysis is done based on the nature of the account of the respondents and customers perceptions with respect to the benefits of BPR and presented in the table below -

Table 5.15F

The type of account vs. Customers perceptions on benefits of BPR services

S.No.	Particulars	Savings Account		Current Account	
		AS	Rank	AS	Rank
1	Time Saving	10.06	1	10.56	1
2	Fastness in Services	8.3	2	9.04	2
3	Home Banking Facilities	4.31	9	8.2	3
4	Easy payments of dues through bank	5.65	4	7.28	6
5	Transparency in facilities	4.57	7	7.72	4
6	Better transfer of funds	4.52	8	4.12	11
7	Easy Clearances	4.64	6	5.64	8
8	Easy balance enquiry	6.37	3	6.32	7
9	Round the clock services	5.41	5	7.44	5
10	Minimizing chances of fraud	2.79	10	3.44	12
11	Hassle free in handling of cash	3.03	11.5	4.96	9
12	Improved customer services	3.03	11.5	4.80	10

Source : Primary data

From the above table we find that the saving account holders have considered easy balance enquiry, easy payment of dues through banks, round the clock services as few other benefits apart from time saving and fastness in services .Current account holders have rated home banking facilities, transparency of facilities and round the clock services as third, fourth and fifth benefits of BPR in order of their ranking.

5.15G Income vs. Customers perceptions on benefits of BPR services :

Analysis is done based on the income of the respondents and customers perceptions with respect to the benefits of BPR and presented in the table below-

Table 5.15G

Income vs. Customers perceptions on benefits of BPR services

S.No.	Particulars	Less than Rs.5 lacs		Rs.5 to 10 lakhs		Above 10 lakhs	
		AS	Rank	AS	Rank	AS	Rank
1	Time Saving	9.97	1	10.48	1	11.38	1
2	Fastness in Services	8.17	2	8.68	2	9.87	3
3	Home Banking Facilities	4.06	7	5.30	9	10.5	2
4	Easy payments of dues through bank	4.87	5	6.73	4	8.50	4.5
5	Transparency in facilities	3.37	9	5.89	6	8.5	4.5
6	Better transfer of funds	3.38	8	5.85	7	6.0	6
7	Easy Clearances	4.44	6	5.37	8	4.50	7.5
8	Easy balance enquiry	6.23	3	6.76	3	4.5	7.5
9	Round the clock services	4.99	4	6.27	5	4.25	9
10	Minimizing chances of fraud	2.40	12	3.86	11	3.75	10
11	Hassle free in handling of cash	2.85	11	4.24	10	2.0	11
12	Improved customer services	3.29	10	3.61	12	1.0	12

Source : Primary data

Respondents with less than Rs. 5 lakhs and between Rs. 5 lakhs to 10 lakhs as their annual income rated time saving and fastness in services and easy balance enquiry as the top three benefits of BPR to customers whereas respondents with annual income of more than Rs.10 lakhs have considered time saving and home banking facilities and fastness in services as the top three benefits of BPR.

5.16 Problems of BPR in banks :

Having examined the responses of customers about the benefits of BPR, an attempt is made here to understand the perception of customers about the problems faced by them after implementation of BPR in banks. For this purpose the respondents are asked to identify the problems and rank them in order of their priority. Further scores were assigned to these ranks as follows :

Ranks	1	2	3	4	5	6	7
Weights	7	6	5	4	3	2	1

The weighted scores and the ranks are shown in table 5.16.

Table No. 5.16

Problems of BPR in banks

S.No.	Particulars	W.S	Ranks
1	Security	1194	3
2	Machine Failures	1414	1
3	Lack of computer	914	4
4	Increase in Service charges	1363	2
5	Loosing personal contact with bank staff	820	5
6	Electricity disturbances	817	6
7	Absence of special issues	505	7

Source : Primary data

It may be observed from the above table that "Machine failures" is ranked as a major problem followed by "Increase in service charges", "Security concerns problems", "Lack of computer knowledge" and so on.

The following conclusions are drawn after carefully examining the customer's perceptions on impact BPR at SBH :

1. It is found that customers perceived "Better Customer Service (20%)"as the primary objective of BPR in banks followed by , "Anywhere banking (17%)", and speedy operations (14%)" as few other major objectives of BPR in banks.
2. It may be concluded that most of the customers (42.8%) visit once in a month, followed by once in a week (36.4%), and daily (12.4%).
3. We can conclude that BPR has resulted in saving time in all the banking transactions under study such as depositing cash in the bank, withdrawal of cash, issue of DD, Opening of new accounts, clearance of cheques etc.

4. There is high level of satisfaction among the respondents with respect to BPR initiatives at SBH (Average Score being 3.09 on a 5 point scale). Highest satisfaction is noticed in case of ATM/Debit card services followed by Multi-Service on a single counter, Credit card service, anywhere banking and other services.

5. It is found that the sample customers feel that the impact of BPR is much "on customers" (4.05) followed by "Banks performance" (3.92) and "on employees" (3.91) .On the whole we can conclude that customers are more satisfied due to BPR in banks.

6. It is found that the lowest percentage of awareness among respondents is with respect to Grahak Mitras, a front office initiative for guiding the customers in conducting their transactions smoothly and helping them in choosing alternate delivery channels like ATM cards, internet banking, etc.

7. We can conclude that about that 78.6% of the respondents are aware of the use of drop boxes facility and 63% of them are using the same.

8. Majority of the respondents felt that "Time Savings" is top most benefit, followed by "fastness in service"," round the clock service" ,easy payments of dues through bank, easy balance enquiry, home banking facilities etc.

9. It may be concluded that "Machine failures" is ranked as a major problem followed by "Increase in service charges", "Security concerns problems", "Lack of computer knowledge" etc due to implementation of BPR at SBH.

To evaluate the impact of Business process Re- Engineering on customer satisfaction in banks the following hypothesis are formulated.

Hypotheses 8

The frequency of visit by the respondents to the bank is independent of the demographic variables of the respondent.

a. There is no significant relationship between occupation of the respondents and the frequency of visit to the bank.

b. There is no significant relationship between income of the respondents and the frequency of visit to the bank.

c. There is a significant relationship between age, gender, occupation, educational qualification, and knowledge of computer skills of the respondents and the frequency of visit to the bank.

Hypotheses 9

The customers' level of satisfaction of BPR at SBH is independent of the demographic variables of the respondent.

a. Further to study whether the age of the respondents are independent of the level of satisfaction of the various BPR initiatives, chi-square test was calculated. It was found that there is no significant relationship between age and the various services such as Multi – Service on a single counter, ATM/ Debit Card Service, anywhere banking, internet banking, fund transfer and e-cheque (.011,006,.002,.000,.002,.038). Whereas, the study indicates that there is a significant relationship between age of the respondents and credit card services (.212).

b. The study reveals that there is no significant relationship between gender of the respondents and the multi service on single counter (chi square test p- value is .005). It was also found that there is a significant relationship between gender and the various services such as ATM/ Debit Card Service, credit card services, anywhere banking, internet banking, fund transfer and e-cheque (.928, .944, .388, 315, .315, .402).

c. To study whether the education qualification of the respondents are independent of the level of satisfaction of the various BPR initiatives, chi-square test was calculated. And it was found that there is no significant relationship between educational qualification of the respondent and the various services such as, ATM/ Debit Card Service, credit card services, anywhere banking, fund transfer (.018, .000, .009, and .001). Whereas, the study further indicates that there is a significant relationship between educational qualification of the respondents and services such as Multi – Service on a single counter, internet banking, and e-cheque (.396, .818, and .204).

d. The study reveals that there is no significant relationship between annual income of the respondents and the fund transfer and e-cheque services (chi square test p- value is .000, .003). It was also found that there is a significant relationship between annual income of the respondents and the various services such as multi service on single counter, ATM/ Debit Card Service, credit card services, anywhere banking, and internet banking, (.157, .348, .280, .284, and .327).

e. Further to study whether the nature of account of the respondents are independent of the level of satisfaction of the various BPR initiatives, chi-square tests were calculated. It was found that there is no significant relationship between nature of account and the various services such as Multi – Service on a single counter, credit card services, internet banking, and fund transfer (.003, .014, .000, .058). Whereas, the study indicates that there is a significant relationship between the nature of account of the respondents and satisfaction of the customers with respect to services such as ATM/ Debit Card Service, anywhere banking, and e-cheque (.504, .519, and .560).

f. The study reveals that there is no significant relationship between the knowledge of computer skills of the respondents and the services such as fund transfer and e-cheque services (chi square test p- value is .001, .012). It was also found that there is a significant relationship between knowledge of computer skills of the respondents and the various services such as multi service on single counter, ATM/ Debit Card Service, credit card services, anywhere banking, and internet banking, (.743, .312, .144, .069, and .078).

Hypotheses 10

The Customers perceptions about impact of BPR on stakeholders (customers, employees and bank), is independent of the demographic variables of the respondent.

a. We can conclude that there is no significant relationship between the age of the respondents and the impact of BPR.

b. The study further confirms that there is a significant relationship of the gender of the respondents and the impact of BPR (0.755, 0.268, and 0.352)

c. We can conclude that there is significant relationship between the educational qualification of the respondents and the impact of BPR on customers. At the same we find that there is no significant relationship between the educational qualification of the respondents and the impact of BPR on employees and on bank performance.

d. We can further conclude that there is significant relationship between the knowledge of computer skills of the respondents and the impact of BPR on customers and on bank performance (0.450 and 0.091). At the same we find that there is no significant relationship between the knowledge of computer skills of the respondents and the impact of BPR on employees (0.030)

e. We can conclude that there is significant relationship between the occupation of the respondents and the impact of BPR on customers (chi-square p value is 0.316). At the same we find that there is no significant relationship between the occupation of the respondents and the impact of BPR on employees and on bank performance (chi-square p value is 0.000 & 0.012).

f. We can conclude that there is no significant relationship between the annual income of the respondents and the impact of BPR on customers. At the same we find that there is a significant relationship between the annual income of the respondents and the impact of BPR on employees and on bank performance.

g. We can conclude that there is significant relationship between the nature of account of the respondents and the impact of BPR on customers and on employees. At the same we find that there is no significant relationship between the nature of account of the respondents and the impact of BPR on bank performance.

Suggestions :

- ATM/Debit card facilities are used widely by the customers, they should reengineer the process of ATM's even for deposit of cash at ATM's, which will reduce turn- around time of customers.
- A customer complaint cell should be established at every branch, so as to enable the customers to express their grievances and solve their problems.
- Management should take the feedback of employees and customers frequently so as to know the pulse of the major stakeholders.
- As the study reveals that the customer awareness of BPR initiatives is low, efforts should be made to bring awareness among customers about the same. (It was revealed from the study that most of the customers are not aware of even grahak mitras).

❖ ❖ ❖

CHAPTER - VI
CONCLUSIONS AND SUGGESTIONS

ANNEXURE - I

BUSINESS PROCESS RE-ENGINEERING IN COMMERCIAL BANKS :

A CASE STUDY OF STATE BANK OF HYDERABAD

QUESTIONNAIRE

Respected Sir/Madam,

Information Technology has basically been used under two different avenues in Banking Sector. One is Communication and Connectivity and other is Business Process Reengineering. One of the key challenges which the banks are facing is the assimilation of new processes and reengineering of existing processes. BPR is 'transformation' as opposed to 'change' that alters the basic rhythm and character of the organization. And this prompts the banks to reengineer the processes so as to comply with these changes.

Hence a study is undertaken on the theme of "BPR in Commercial Banks - A case study of SBH, as a part of Doctoral programme registered in the Department of Commerce, Osmania University, Hyderabad, to examine the status of BPR in commercial Banks and its impact on the employees and also the organizational change in their Banks.

We request you to kindly spare your valuable time in filling this questionnaire, your valuable inputs and cooperation will go a long way in furthering the cause of academic excellence in general and excellence of the banking industry in particular.

Please note that this survey is being conducted purely in the interest of academic research and is not funded by any commercial organization or initiative. Thus your information will be kept confidential and will be used purely for academic purpose. At the end of the study we will send you a copy of summery report if required.

Thanking you,

Yours faithfully,

Prof. S.V.Satyanarayana,
Research Guide,
Deapartment of Commerce,
Osmania University,
Hyderabad -500007.

N.V.Kavitha,
Research Scholar.

BUSINESS PROCESS RE-ENGINEERING IN COMMERCIAL BANKS : A CASE STUDY OF STATE BANK OF HYDERABAD

QUESTIONNAIRE

PART – I

Employee Profile

1. Name (If Desired) :

2. Designation :

3. Age :

S. No.	Particulars	Response
1	Below 25 years	( )
2	25yrs to 50 years	( )
3	Above 50 years	( )

4. Sex :

S. No.	Particulars	Response
1	Male	( )
2	Female	( )

5. Educational Qualification :

S. No.	Particulars	Response
1	SSC and below	( )
2	Graduate	( )
3	Post Graduate and above	( )

6. Computer Skills :

S. No.	Particulars	Response
1	Software	( )
2	Hardware	( )

7. Experience in the Bank (No of Years of service) :

S. No.	Particulars	Response
1	Less than 5 years	( )
2	5 to 10 years	( )
3	Above 10 years	( )

8. Annual Income :

S. No.	Particulars	Response
1	Less than Rs. 5 lakhs	( )
2	Rs. 5 lakhs to Rs. 10 lakhs	( )
3	Above Rs. 10 lakhs	( )

PART – II

EMPLOYEES PERCEPTION ON BUSINESS PROCESS RE-ENGINEERING AT STATE BANK OF HYDERABAD

1. In your opinion what are the objectives of business process reengineering in your bank?

Rank the objectives according to your own perception from 1 to 12.

S.No.	Particulars	Response
1	Cost reduction in operations	( )
2	Accuracy of transactions	( )
3	Speedy operations	( )
4	Better customer services	( )
5	Adoption of latest technology	( )
6	Reducing cost of employees	( )
7	Reduction of staff	( )
8	Easy rectification of errors	( )
9	To satisfy existing customers	( )
10	To create new customers	( )
11	To win over competitors	( )
12	Please specify if any other	( )

2. Please indicate your awareness regarding following. Tick the appropriate with (✔)

S.No.	Particulars	Response		
		Fully Aware	Partly Aware	Not Aware
1	Back-end software used for banking operations			
2	Recommendations of Information technology in the banks			
3	Knowledge about electronic services offered by banks			
4	Hardware knowledge to correct simple technical snags			
5	Retail banking i.e. CPC's			
6	Core sales and service branch - SSB			
7	Product and customer centric sales force			
8	Alternate delivery channels			

3. Indicate your level of agreement regarding the impact of information technology on bank employees for the following :

1 = Strongly disagree, 2 = Disagree, 3 = Neither agree nor disagree, 4 = Agree, 5 = Strongly Agree

S. No.	Particulars	Response				
		1	2	3	4	5
1	BPR in banks does not help to improve efficiency of employees.					
2	It is difficult for the employees to switch over from manual system to computerized system.					
3	Most of the bank employees took VRS on account of re-engineering of processes in banks					
4	The bank employees are overburdened after BPR in banks.					
5	We are losing face to face contact with customers an account of BPR in banks					
6	There is a threat on status of employees due to BPR in the banks.					

4. In your opinion, what are the benefits to the bank employees on account of business process reengineering in the banks? Rank the benefits according to your own perception from 1 to 10.

S.No.	Particulars	Response
1	Faster customer service	( )
2	Reduce transaction errors and misunderstandings	( )
3	Lower transmission costs	( )
4	Greater efficiency	( )
5	Easy clearance	( )
6	Time saving	( )
7	Increase in the no of banking services	( )
8	Retaining existing customers	( )
9	Provides better management information	( )
10	Increase in transaction volume	( )

5. What are the problems faced by the bank employees on account of recent Changes. (Indicate 1, 2, 3, ... in order of preference)

S.No.	Particulars	Response
1	Lack of trained personnel	( )
2	Loss of brain power	( )
3	Security concern problems	( )
4	Machine failures	( )
5	Data integrity problems	( )
6	Threat to status of employees	( )
7	Threat to ego for employees	( )
8	Threat to security for employees	( )
9	Electricity disturbances	( )
10	Please specify if any other	( )

6. Indicate the level of your satisfaction on the following after the recent initiatives made in your banks. 1 = highly satisfied, 2 = Satisfied, 3 = neither satisfied nor dissatisfied, 4 = dissatisfied, 5 = highly dissatisfied

S.No.	Particulars	Response				
		1	2	3	4	5
1	Work load					
2	Extra allowance					
3	Recognition					
4	Promotion opportunities					
5	Salary and monetary benefits					
6	Job security					
7	Please specify if any other					

7. How do you rate the impact of business processes reengineering on banks?

   1. High Impact, 2.Moderate, 3. Little impact, 4. No impact, 5. Adverse impact

S.No.	Particulars	Response				
1	On Customers	1	2	3	4	5
2	On Employees	1	2	3	4	5
3	On bank Performance	1	2	3	4	5

8. Please give reasons for your response

   -------------------------.

9. In your opinion , what is the level of your satisfaction in the banking services after BPR in the banks? 1 = highly satisfied, 2 = Satisfied, 3 = neither satisfied nor dissatisfied, 4 = dissatisfied, 5 = highly dissatisfied

S.No.	Particulars	Response				
		1	2	3	4	5
1	Cash payments					
2	Cash receipts					
3	Printed statements of various accounts					
4	Issue of cheque book					
5	Issue of drafts					
6	Fund transfer					

7	Disbursement of loans					
8	Multi – service on a single counter					
9	ATM cum Debit card facilities					
10	Credit card management					
11	Internet banking					
12	Drop boxes					

10. How do you rate the customer services for the following before and after computerization/ Indicate your response with 1 = good, 2 = Average, 3 = Poor.

S.No.	Transaction	Before 2005	After 2005
1	Cash withdrawal	( )	( )
3	Deposit of cash	( )	( )
4	Opening a new account :	( )	( )
5	Obtaining demand draft or pay order	( )	( )
6	Updating the pass book :	( )	( )
7	Calculation of product interest on the balance	( )	( )
8	Clearance of outstation cheques /DD's	( )	( )
9	Inter branch reconciliation	( )	( )
10	Furnishing of bank statements to the customers	( )	( )

Thank you

ANNEXURE – II

BUSINESS PROCESS RE-ENGINEERING IN COMMERCIAL BANKS: A CASE STUDY OF STATE BANK OF HYDERABAD

Questionnaire for Customers

Respected Sir/Madam,

Information Technology has basically been used under two different avenues in Banking Sector. One is Communication and Connectivity and other is Business Process Reengineering. One of the key challenges which the banks are facing is the assimilation of new processes and reengineering of existing processes. BPR is 'transformation' as opposed to 'change' that alters the basic rhythm and character of the organization. And this prompts the banks to reengineer the processes so as to comply with these changes.

Hence a study is undertaken on the theme of "BPR in Commercial Banks – A case study of SBH, as a part of Doctoral programme registered in the Department of Commerce, Osmania University, Hyderabad, to examine the impact of BPR on customer satisfaction in banks.

We request you to kindly spare your valuable time in filling this questionnaire, your valuable inputs and cooperation will go a long way in furthering the cause of academic excellence in general and excellence of the banking industry in particular.

Please note that this survey is being conducted purely in the interest of academic research and is not funded by any commercial organization or initiative. Thus your information will be kept confidential and will be used purely for academic purpose.

Thanking you,

Yours faithfully,

Prof. S.V.Satyanarayana,
Research Guide,
Deapartment of Commerce,
Osmania University,
Hyderabad -500007.

N.V.Kavitha,
Research Scholar.

BUSINESS PROCESS RE-ENGINEERING IN COMMERCIAL BANKS: A CASE STUDY OF STATE BANK OF HYDERABAD

QUESTIONNAIRE

PART – I

Customers Profile

1. Name (If Desired) :

2. Age :

S.No.	Particulars	Response
1	Below 25 years	( )
2	25yrs to 50 years	( )
3	Above 50 years	( )

3. Sex :

S.No.	**Particulars**	**Response**
1	Male	( )
2	Female	( )

4. Educational Qualification :

S. No.	**Particulars**	**Response**
1	SSC and below	( )
2	Graduate	( )
3	Post graduate and above	( )

5. Computer Skills : YES/NO

6. Occupation : Business/Employment/Profession/Others

7. Annual Income :

S. No.	**Particulars**	**Response**
1	Less than Rs.5lakhs	( )
2	Rs. 5 lakhs to Rs.10lakhs	( )
3	Above Rs. 10 lakhs	( )

8. Type of Account opened :

S. No.	Particulars	Response
1	Savings Account	( )
2	Current Account	( )
3	**Any other Account**	( )

PART – II

EMPLOYEES PERCEPTION ON BUSINESS PROCESS RE-ENGINEERING AT STATE BANK OF HYDERABAD

1. In your opinion what are the objectives of business process reengineering in your bank? Tick the appropriate with (✔)

S.No.	Particulars	Response
1	Anywhere Banking	
2	Faster and efficient customer service	
3	Reducing the operational cost	
4	Offering multiple delivery channels	
5	Centralizing the bank end processes	
6	Creating a customer profile database	
7	To enhance quality of customer service	
8	Speedy operations	
9	To create new customers	
10	Please specify if any other	

2. Indicate the order of preference the purpose of visiting the bank

(Indicate 1, 2, 3, ... in order of preference)

S.No.	Particulars	Response
1	Deposit / Withdrawal of cash	
2	Demand draft / Pay order	
3	Credit Card Transactions	
4	Updating the Pass book	
5	Cash credit Operations	
6	Locker facilities	
7	Availing Loan services	
8	Any other (specify)	

3. Indicate the frequency of your visit to the bank

S.No.	Particulars	Response
1	Daily	
2	Once in a week	
3	Once in a month	
4	Once in three months	

4. Kindly furnish the approximate time taken for each of the following transactions before 2005 and after 2005. Tick the appropriate with (✔)

S.No	Transaction	Before 2005	After 2005
1	Cash withdrawal :		
	a) Less than 15 minutes	( )	( )
	b) 15 to 30 minutes	( )	( )
	c) More than 30 minutes	( )	( )
2	Withdrawal through cheques:		
	a) Less than 15 minutes	( )	( )
	b) 15 to 30 minutes	( )	( )
	c) More than 30 minutes	( )	( )
3	Deposit of cash :		
	a) Less than 15 minutes	( )	( )
	b) 15 to 30 minutes	( )	( )
	c) More than 30 minutes	( )	( )
4	Time spent in opening a new account :		
	a) Less than 15 minutes	( )	( )
	b) 15 to 30 minutes	( )	( )
	c) More than 30 minutes	( )	( )
5	Obtaining demand draft or pay order :		
	a) Less than 15 minutes	( )	( )
	b) 15 to 30 minutes	( )	( )
	c) More than 30 minutes	( )	( )
6	Time spent on updating the pass book :		
	a) Less than 15 minutes	( )	( )
	b) 15 to 30 minutes	( )	( )
	c) More than 30 minutes	( )	( )

7	Clearance of local cheques : a) Less than 3 days b) 3 to 5 days c) More than 5 days	( ) ( ) ( )	( ) ( ) ( )
8	Clearance of outstation cheques : a) Less than 10 days b) 10 to 20 days c) More than 20 days	( ) ( ) ( )	( ) ( ) ( )

5. Please indicate your awareness and usage of the following services provided by the bank.

   Tick the appropriate with (✔)

S.No.	Banking Services	Aware	Usage
1	Cash withdrawals	( )	( )
2	Cash Deposits	( )	( )
3	Demand Drafts/ Pay Orders	( )	( )
4	Cheque Deposits	( )	( )
5	ATM/Debit Card facilities	( )	( )
6	Credit Card Facilities	( )	( )
7	Grahak Mitras	( )	( )
8	Drop Boxes	( )	( )
9	Loker Facilities	( )	( )
10	Loans	( )	( )
11	Internet Banking	( )	( )
12	Anywhere Banking	( )	( )
13	Fund tranfer	( )	( )
14	Foreign Exchange	( )	( )
15	Any Other (specify)	( )	( )

6. In your opinion, what is the level of satisfaction for banking services on account of the computerization in the banks?

   The question is measured on a five point scale .Please indicate how strongly you agree or disagree with each of the following scale : ***1 = highly satisfied, 2 = Satisfied, 3 = neither satisfied nor dissatisfied, 4 = dissatisfied, 5 = highly dissatisfied***

S.No.	Particulars	Response				
1	Multi – Service on a single counter	1	2	3	4	5
2	ATM/ Debit Card Service	1	2	3	4	5
3	Credit Card Service	1	2	3	4	5
4	Anywhere Banking	1	2	3	4	5
5	Internet Banking	1	2	3	4	5
6	Fund Transfer	1	2	3	4	5
7	E- Cheque	1	2	3	4	5

7. Indicate the reasons for dissatisfaction, if any, for the above services.

----

8. How do you rate the impact of business processes reengineering on banks?

1. High Impact, 2. Moderate, 3. Little impact, 4. No impact, 5. Adverse impact

S.No.	Particulars	Response				
1	On Customers	1	2	3	4	5
2	On Employees	1	2	3	4	5
3	On bank Performance	1	2	3	4	5

9. In your opinion, what are the benefits to the customers on account of BPR in the banks? (Indicate 1, 2, 3, …… in order of preference)

S.No.	Particulars	Response
1	Time Saving	
2	Fastness in Services	
3	Home Banking Facilities	
4	Easy payments of dues through bank	
5	Transparency in facilities	
6	Better transfer of funds	
7	Easy Clearances	

8	Easy balance enquiry	
9	Round the clock services	
10	Minimizing chances of fraud	
11	Hassle free in handling of cash	
12	Improved customer services	

10. In your opinion, what are the problems faced by the customers on account of BPR

(Indicate 1, 2, 3 … in order of preference)

S.No.	Particulars	Response
1	Security	
2	Machine Failures	
3	Lack of computer	
4	Increase in Service charges	
5	Loosing personal contact with bank staff	
6	Electricity disturbances	
7	Absence of special issues	
8	Any Other (specify)	

Thank you

BIBLIOGRAPHY

1. Aggarwal, H.N. (1979), A Portrait of Nationalized Banks- A study with reference to their social obligations. (New Delhi: Inter-India Publications).

2. Adhivarahan, V. (2001), 'Information Technology Act, 2000- The Legal Viewpoint'. Indian Banking Association, Bulletin, Vol.XXII No. 12 (Dec.).

3. Amandeep, (1983), Profits and Profitability in Commercial Banks (New Delhi: Deep & Deep Publications).

4. Angadi & Devraj, (1983), 'Profitability and Productivity of Banks in India'. Economic and Political Weekly, Vol. 18 (Nov. 26).

5. Avasthi, G.P. and Sharma, M. (2000-2001), 'Information Technology in Banking: Challenges for Regulators', Prajnan, Vol. XXIX, No. 4 p-17.

6. Berman, Saul, Strategic Direction: Don't Reengineer Without It; Scanning the Horizon for Turbulence, Planning Review, November 1994; Pg. 18.

7. B.Janki, (2002), 'Unleashing Employee Productivity: Need for a Paradigm Shift'. Indian Banking Association Bulletin, Vol. XXIV No.3 (March). PP 7-9.

8. Bajaj, K.K. (2000), 'E-Commerce Issues in the Emerging Hi-Tech. Banking Environment'. The Journal of The Indian Institute of Bankers, (Jan-March).

9. Bajaj, K.K. (1999), E-Commerce, The Cutting Edge of Business. (New Delhi: Tata McGraw Hill Publ. Company Ltd.).

10. Benton, E. (1990), Bank Fraud: Exposing the Hidden Threat to Financial Institutions. (McGraw-Hill Companies).

11. Bhasin, T.M. (2001): E-Commerce In Indian Banking Indian Banking Association Bulletin, Vol.XXIII Nos. 4 & 5 (April-May)

12. Bhattacharya, A (1997), 'The Impact of Liberalisation on the Productive Efficiency of Indian Commercial Banks', European Journal of Operational Research 98, pp. 332-

13. Bhunia, C.T. (2000), 'Coming Soon Internet'. Electronics for You, (Jan.).

14. Bilgarni, S.A.R. (1982), Growth of Public Sector- A Regional Growth Analysis. (New Delhi: Deep and Deep Publications).

15. Birla Institute of Scientific Research, (1981), Banks Since Nationalization. New Delhi: Allied Publishers Pvt. Ltd.).

16. Brett, F. Woods. (1997), E-Money: Financial Management in the Electronic Age. (Paladin Press).

17. Brown, Tom, De-engineering the Corporation, Industry Week, April 18, 1994; Pg. 18.

18. Banerjee Abhijit V., Shawn Cole and Esther Duflo, 2004. Banking Reform in India, *MIMEO*, MIT.

19. Berger, A.N. and Humphrey, D.B. (1997). Efficiency of financial institutions: international survey and directions for future research, *European Journal of Operational Research*, 98, 175-212.

20. Bhattacharyya, A., Lovell, C.A.K. and Sahay, P. (1997). The impact of liberalization on the productive efficiency of Indian commercial banks, *European Journal of Operational Research*, 98, 332-345.

21. Bhaumik, Sumon K. and Jenifer Piesse, 2003. Are foreign banks active in emerging credit markets? Evidence from the Indian banking industry, *Working Paper*,Queen's University, Belfast.

22. Cafasso, Rosemary, Rethinking Reengineering, Computerworld, March 15, 1993; Pg. 102.

23. Caldwell, Bruce, Missteps, Miscues – Business Reengineering Failures, InformationWeek, June 20, 1994; Pg. 50.

24. Chew, Angie, How Insurance Firms Can Reengineer for Success, Business Times, June 20, 1994; Pg. 11.

25. Chakravarty, T.K. (1986), 'Profitability of Banks: An empirical attempt for identification of variable of income and expendciture of scheduled commercial banks for Profit Planning.' Paper presented to the Bank Economist Meet, pp 3.17 to 3.61.

26. Casu, Barbara, Claudia Girardone and Philip Molyneux, 2004, Productivity change inEuropean banking: A comparison of parametric and non-parametric approaches,*Journal of Banking & Finance,* Vol 28, Issue 10, Pp. 2521-2540

27. Chopra, K. (1987), Managing Profitability and Productivity in Public Sector Banking, (Jalandhar: ABS Publ.)

28. Clifford E. Kirsch. (1996), The Financial Services Revolution: Understanding the Changing Roles of Banks, Mutual Funds, and Insurance Companies. (McGraw-Hill Companies).

29. Cone, Edward, Technology Chief of the Year; All the Right Moves – Tom Trainer of Reebok International Successfully Teamed Business Reengineering with Information Technology, InformationWeek, December 26, 1994; Pg. 35.

30. Davenport, Thomas H., Will Participative Makeovers of Business Processes Succeed Where Reengineering Failed? Planning Review, January 1995; Pg. 24.

31. Das, A. (1999), 'Profitability of Public Sector Banks: A Decompostion Model", RBI Occasional Papers 20, 1.

32. D'Souza, Errol, 2002. How Well Have Public Sector Banks Done? A Note. *Economicand Political Weekly*, March 2, 2002.

33. Das, Abhiman, 2002. Risk and Productivity Change of Public Sector Banks, *and Political Weekly*, February 2, 2002

34. Economist Newspaper Group, Reengineering Reviewed, The Economist, June 1994, Pg 24.

35. Ettorre, Barbara, Reengineering Tales from the Front, Management Review, January 1995; Pg. 13.

36. Federick F. Reichheld & Phil. S. (2000), 'E-Loyalty' Harvard Business Review (July-Aug.).

37. Galagadera, Don U.A. and P. Edirisuriya, 2004, Performance of Indian commercial banks(1995-2002): an application of data envelopment analysis and Malmquistproductivity index, *Working Paper*, Monash University.

38. Gupta, Nandini, 2005, Partial Privatization and Firm Performance, *The Journal of Finance*, Vol. LX, No. 2, pp. 987-1015.

39. Godse, V.J. (1983), 'Looking A fresh At Banking Productivity', Selected Readings On Productivity, The Times Research Foundation, Bombay, PP 137 to 148.

40. Gupta, M. & Goswami, S. (1986), 'Profitability and Profit Planning in Banks Establishment Cost And Stff Strength', Paper presented to the Bank Economist Meet, pp. 3.92 to 3.100.

41. Heggade, O.D. (2000), Banker-Customer Relationship in India. (New Delhi : Mohit Publications).

42. Hussain, F. (1988), Computerization and Mechanization in Indian Banks (New Delhi : Deep & Deep Publications).

43. Johri and Jauhari, (1994), Role of Computers in Banking Operation Systems. (New Delhi : Himalaya Publ. House).

44. Joshi, P.N. (1986), 'Profitability and Profit Planning in Banks, Bankers Economists Meet.

45. Furey, Tim R. and Garlitz, Jennifer L. and Kelleher, Michael L., Applying Information Technology to Reengineering, Planning Review, November 1993; Pg. 22.

46. Hamel, Gary and Prahalad, C.K., Competing for the Future, Harvard Business Review, July-August 1994; Pg. 122.

47. Hyatt, Joshua, Real-World Reengineering, Inc., April 1995; Pg. 42.

48. Janson, Robert, How Reengineering Transforms Organizations to Satisfy Customers, National Productivity Review, December 22, 1992; Pg. 45

49. Karkal, G.L. (1982), 'Profits and Profitability in Banking,' IBA Bulletin, Vol. XXIII No. 3 (March).

50. Kaveri, V.S. (2001), 'Loan Default and Profitability of Banks'. IBA Bulletin, Vol.XXIII No. 1 (Jan.)

51. Kao, Chiang and Shiang- Tai Liu, 2004, Predicting bank performance with financial forecasts: A case of Taiwan commercial banks, *Journal of Banking & Finance,* Vol 28, Issue 10, Pages 2353-2368

52. Koeva, Petya, 2003. The Performance of Indian Banks During Financial Liberalzation, *IMF Working Paper* No. 03/150.

53. Kumbhakar, S.C. and Sarkar, S. (2003). Deregulation, ownership, and productivity growth in the banking industry: evidence from India, *Journal of Money, Credit, and Banking*, 35, 403-424.

54. Kohli, S.S. (2001), Indian Banking Industry: Emerging Challenges'. IBA Bulletin, Vol. XXIII No. (March).

55. Kavanagh, John, Challenge for Company Culture - Business Reengineering: The Need for Totally New Thinking, The Financial Times, March 23, 1993, Survey of Information and Communications Technology (19); Pg. IX.

56. Kehoe, Louise, Down in the Dirt to Clean Up IBM/ Louise Kehoe Offers a Contrasting View of Business Process Re- engineering, Financial Times, December 5, 1994; Pg. 8.

57. Leth, Steven A., Critical Success Factors for Reengineering Business Processes, National Productivity Review, September 22, 1994; Pg. 557.

58. Lloyd, Tom, Giant with Feet of Clay/ Tom Lloyd Offers a Contrasting View of Business Process Reengineering, Financial Times, December 5, 1994; Pg. 8.

59. Lorenz, Christopher, Reengineering in Small Doses Only, The Financial Times, July 1, 1994; Pg. 14.

60. Mampilly, P. (1980), 'Innovations in Banking: The Indian experience, Cost and Profitability of Commercial Banking'. Development and Economics Deppt., World Bank.

61. Murty, P.V.R., (1996), Cost and Profitability of Public Sector Banks.

62. Murty, G.R.K., (2001), 'Banks Foray into Insurance: The Road Ahead'. IBA Bulletin, Vol. XXIII No. 10 (Oct.

63. Mukherjee, K., S. C. Ray and S. M. Miller, 2001, Productivity growth in large US commercial banks: The initial post-deregulation experience, *Journal of Banking & Finance,* Vol 25, Issue 5, Pages 913-939

64. May, Thornton, Not-So-Successful Reengineering, Byte, December 1994; Pg. 45.

65. Moad, Jeff, After Reengineering: Taking Care of Business, Datamation, October 15, 1994; Pg. 40.

66. Moad, Jeff, Does Reengineering Really Work? Datamation, August 1, 1993; Pg. 22.

67. Schnitt, David L., Reengineering the Corporation Using Information Technology, Journal of Systems Management, January 1993; Pg. 14.

68. Strassman, Paul A., The Rap on Reengineering, Computerworld, September 26, 1994; Pg. 119.

69. Sabnani, P. (2000), 'Universal Banking', IBA Bulletin, Vol.XXII No. 7 (July).

70. Sachdeva, U.S. (1987), Frauds and Banks : Prevention and Detection Techniques. (New Delhi : UDH Publ. House).

71. Sadare, A.M. (1984), 'Some Issues in Measurement of Productivity in Commercial Banks', Bank Economists Meet, pp. 275-285.

72. Sarker, P.C. and Das, A. (1997), 'Development of Composite Index of Banking Efficiency : The Indian Case'. RBI Occasional Papers 18, 1.

73. Satyamurty, B. (1994), 'A Study on Interest Spread in Commercial Banks in India', NIBM, Working Paper.

74. Saxena, M. (2001), 'Bankers' Choice : Tech it or Leave it,' Strategic Marketing, (Feb.), pp.42-50.

75. Shah, S.G. (1977), 'Bank Personal : Manpower for Banking Productivity,' Commerce (Sept.,24).

76. Shah, V.D. (1986), 'Empirical Relationship Between Size and Cost and Branch level,' Prajanan, Vol. XV No. 318 (Janu.-March), pp.29-48.

77. Shanti, S. (1984), Customer Services in Banks. (Bombay : Himalaya Publication House).

78. Shapiro, C. (2000), 'Will E-Commerce Erode Liberty,' Harvard Business Review (May-June).

79. Shastri, R.V. (2001), 'Technology for Banks in India Challenges,' IBA Bulletin, Vol. XXIII No. 3 (March).

80. Singh,j[1990] , Productivity in the Indian Banking Industry [New Delhi : Deep and Deep publ]

81. Subrahmanyam , G. (1984), 'Some Conceptual Issues in Productivity Measurement' Prajanan. (April-June), pp. 173-185.

82. Sushila, S. (1987), Banks and Customers : A Behavioral Analysis. (New Delhi : Shri Ram Centre for Industrial Relations and Human Resources).

83. Swamy, B.N.A. (2001), 'New Competition, Deregulation and Emerging Changes in Indian Banking : An Analysis of Different Banks – Groups', The Journal of The Indian Institute of Bankers. Vol.72, No. 3 (July- Set.) pp 3-22.

84. Saha, A. and Ravisankar, T.S. (2000). Rating of Indian commercial banks: a DEA approach, *European Journal of Operational Research*, 124, 187-203.

85. Sarkar, Subrata, Jayati Sarkar and Sumon K. Bhaumik, 1998. Does Ownership always Matter? Evidence from the Indian Banking Industry, *Journal of Comparative Economics*, Vol. 26, pp.262-281

86. Sathye, Milind, 2003, Efficiency of banks in a developing economy: The case of India, *European Journal of Operational Research,* Vol. 148, Issue 3, pp. 662-671

87. Taylor, Billy E., Keeping BPR from Being TQMed, Enterprise Reengineering, Jan 1995; Pg. 5.

88. Topalova, Petia, 2004. Overview of the Indian Corporate Sector: 1989-2002. *IMF Working Paper* No. 04/

89. Whiting, John T., Reengineering the Corporation (book review), Industrial Management, November 1994; Pg. 14.

90. Wadikar, S.A. (1980), Private Sector Banking in India since 1969 – A Study in its Operations. Ph.D. Thesis (Unpublished).

91. Zahir, M.A. (1980), Transfer Price Mechanism For Performance Evaluation,' Reading in Management, pp 413-422.

❖ ❖ ❖